REBOOT

70 Life Lessons
with Dallas Willard

To Carl & Rebecca,
You are
an inspiring
couple and
dear friends!
Thanks for
being there
for me so
many times!
Blessings!
Dave

REBOOT

70 Life Lessons
with Dallas Willard

Dana Hanson

ANAHEIM—CALIFORNIA

Reboot:
70 Life Lessons with Dallas Willard
© 2015 by Dana Hanson

ISBN-10: 0-9915447-5-7
ISBN-13: 978-0-9915447-5-2

Cover Artwork © 2015 by Mike Jusko

Copy Editing by Steve Souza

Book Design by César Puch

Good Son Books logo created by Luke Spooner

GOOD SON BOOKS
1854 W. Chateau Ave.
Anaheim, CA 92804
USA

Love your neighbor as yourself.
—*Mark 12:31*

To Nancy.
My closest neighbor.

INTRODUCTION

Why This Book?
Reboot: 70 Life Lessons with Dallas Willard is a daily tool intended as a catalyst for life change aimed at everyday people. We have rare opportunities to have our lives "rebooted" without significant events occurring, positive or negative. What if we could intentionally begin this process at any time? That's what Reboot is all about. God transforming our lives. Changing us from the inside out. Along with Dallas' writings, author Dana Hanson, a long-time personal student and friend of Dallas relies heavily on the influence of personal conversations… In clear and concise daily words, Dana invites the reader to join him in reboot, open to the guidance of the Holy Spirit.

Why 10 weeks? Research shows it takes about 10 weeks for a habit to become permanent in our lives. In 70 short, deep, and practical daily writings, Dana provides a framework for anyone open and willing to begin to truly live a life of lasting transformation in God's Gracious Kingdom.

How To Read This Book
This book is organized with a 10 week daily reading and

reflecting approach in mind. It is best to read this book with at least one other person so you can encourage each other and spur each other on in the actions you will be testing out. Then you can discuss how it's going in this journey together.

In a small group, Bible class, one-on-one friendship… whatever configuration you choose…to be learning and practicing with others, joining together with the Trinitarian community of Father, Son and Holy Spirit, will be helpful.

Dana also includes a quote each day from Dallas Willard. These are related to the thought for the day and are drawn mainly from Dana's memory of conversations he had with Dallas over the years. These are some of the nuggets that stuck. The vast majority of these will certainly be included in Dallas' writings.

ACKNOWLEDGEMENTS

To finally get down in writing what I have learned, lived, modeled and taught over the years is a good thing. With a deep gratitude to God for the gift of friendship and influence, Dallas Willard leaves his mark.

I thank Nancy for encouraging me along the way and for being my partner in parenting, and now grandparenting, as we pass down what we have received. Thanks to our kids Kristina, Gregory and David, who have been a sounding board for what is in this book on so many levels. They are so gracious as they, and mom, continue to hear some things "over and over again."

Thanks to those friends who connected me to Dallas and encouraged me along the way, in particular Lynn Corey, Bill Dwyer, and Leroy Chavez. Thanks to those colleague writers who spurred me on to get going on this book (any book!) especially Dave Housholder, Bob Rognlien, Steve Goodwin and Rich Melheim. Thanks to other colleague friends who have been a sounding board on all things Dallas, Mike Anderson, Rich Gregory, Tom Brashears and Sean Kelly.

I am so blessed by my LIFEhouse Church extended family who have faithfully received what I have received and passed it on to others. A special thanks to Buzz Brown who has supported and encouraged getting this message out for many years, and to Mike Jusko, artist extraordinaire, for the cover art.

A heartfelt thank you to Jane Willard who was such an anchor of joy for Dallas and a deep influence on so many as she expands their influence on our lives.

Thanks to Roy Robbins and his team for their work on this book and for bringing it to life.

Finally, thanks to my earthly father and mother who always supported my thirst for knowledge and the things of God, and for my heavenly Father, Son and Holy Spirit for inviting me into their community of love and joy.

FOREWORD

How would you like to meet Dallas?

Little did I know that this simple invitation from my friend Lynn Cory would be like the starting point of the Big Bang, only this was the beginning of God's universe becoming my universe, expanding together.

It all begins in 2000. I am on a pastor's retreat and the topic is Stress and the Ministry. The speaker is giving us key warning signs of being under too much stress, and I am checking off every box. I got that. I got that. I got that.

If this was Bingo it would have been awesome, but it wasn't Bingo. It was me trying to be Mr. Church Growth at the time. I was eating, sleeping, breathing, and strategizing how to get more butts in the seats.

The night before the retreat is over we have Evening Prayer and Healing Service. For Lutherans a healing service often looks like this:

Let's do everything we can not to get too personal about all this healing stuff. We'll say a bunch of generic, written-down prayers, give the option of coming up for personal prayer which is also prewritten and in the book. The key thing is, let's make very sure that everything is done with order and dignity, and make absolutely sure it doesn't get too weird. As a Lutheran Christian wired more experientially, I have never actually used any of these written healing prayer services. I've always been more likely to use free prayer and laying-on-of-hands healing prayer when I am leading worship and prayer.

Well, wouldn't you know it, even with the orderly decorum, the weird happened anyway! This is a beautiful Roman Catholic Retreat Center, in the hills above Santa Barbara. The chapel is medieval; gorgeous with chandeliers for lights. In the middle of worship, a chandelier explodes and sparks shower down from the ceiling! I'm freaking out, but nobody else looks up, including the preacher.

What the heck is going on?

Then it was time for the healing part of the service. I whispered to my friend, Mike, about the chandelier, and he said he saw something, too. No one else we talked to did, however. So, we get in line and wait for prayer.

There are two pastors doing the healing prayer at the front, one of them being the national head bishop of the Lutheran Church at the time, the other a local pastor. The bishop was out visiting from Chicago in February. Interesting how church officials always find a way to get out to California in the winter...Anyway, I choose the bishop's line, and said to my friend, tongue-in-cheek, "I'm going with the bishop 'cause he's got all the power!"

Both of us know I am being a bit facetious, as I am more than slightly suspicious of anything that smacks of hierarchy or pomp in the church. Now it's my turn for prayer, and the bishop quotes Jesus, responding to the blind man on the road to Jericho—

What do you want?

I want peace in my life.

He puts oil on my forehead, lays his hand on my shoulders and begins to pray.

Wham!

A huge surge of Holy Spirit shoots through me! High Voltage!

I didn't fall over or anything. At least I am kneeling already.

After worship, I talked about what happened with Mike, and then some other friends there, and then I returned home, talked to my wife, Nancy, about it.

Before I could get more than a few words out, I burst out crying for over an hour! Just a blubbering mass of tears and sobs. Understand, this wasn't my normal way of saying, "Honey, I'm home!" It seemed to last forever.

Well, that was it. It was like the Holy Spirit is my MMA opponent and he's saying,

You want some of this? I'll give you some of this!

So, from that day on, February 29, 2000, I begin a mixture of fasting and praying and being more intentional in seeking God's guidance in my life.

Even though I am wired pentecostal, at that time I had a hard time processing this, for two reasons. One, I didn't know many pentecostals, and two, because I was a bit of an intellectual snob. Emphasizing the power of the Holy Spirit and deep thinking didn't seem to go together very well with my way of thinking.

Peace did start to arrive, however. Along with the expected attacks by the anti-Prince of Peace. It is rough going and amazing.

Soon, a pastor from nearby Valley Vineyard Church of Reseda, Lynn Corey, calls me out of the blue and tells me he senses God wants him to pray for me. I don't even know this guy, he knows a friend of mine, but I love prayer, so we pray.

This continues over the phone for the next month and then, Bill Dwyer, senior pastor of Valley Vineyard, asks me to speak at one of their weeknight services. They are inviting pastors from other churches to come and share. I accept happily, and meet Bill, and finally Lynn, face-to-face. The spirit of the congregation was warm, potent, gracious and expectant. I teach on evangelism and after the service, Bill has a book in his hand.

"Thanks for coming and I would like to give you this book in appreciation. I think you will enjoy it."

The book was, *The Divine Conspiracy*, by some guy named, Dallas Willard.

I never heard of him.

The book was awarded "Book of the Year" the year before, in 1999, by "Christianity Today" Magazine, but coming out of the Lutheran Church, especially back then, we are pretty picky about what we read. Usually it is something from our own publishing house. I had branched out to others publishers early on but didn't know Dallas Willard.

There is not much written concerning the Holy Spirit or Kingdom theology through our publishers back then, so no Dallas even in footnotes. I thought it would be an interesting read, though. Little did I know.

So, I thanked Bill and Lynn and went home. This was in April, and by the time September rolled around, I had worn that book out. It's as if I had come home. I felt somewhat like the Ethiopian eunuch (Acts 8:31), who is asked if he understands what he is reading.

How can I, unless someone instructs me?

The Divine Conspiracy. Intellectually, more than satisfying, with a heavy emphasis on the Holy Spirit. It's like I had died and gone to heaven. Or, as Dallas would say, "I am coming alive and heaven is coming to me!"

Please understand, this part of my story is repeated in countless lives of so many others around the world. God, working through the pages of this book, and other writings of Dallas Willard, uses him to, indeed, change our thinking.

Now, it is six months later, and I am asked to run for bishop of our synod. Bishop? You've got to be kidding? Along with my aforementioned skepticism, I am more on the conservative side of our denomination in a very left and very blue synod. Actually, I didn't get too involved in any denomination stuff, so am not well known by the other Lutheran church folk, and frankly am not too well respected by the clergy. Not unfairly, I might add. I could be a bit of a jerk with them.

So, I say what any abnormal person would say in this case, Sure, I'll accept your nomination. Then Lynn calls me and senses a word from God that he has something big in store for me soon. I tell him about the bishop nomination. But, at that time, big looked like about 15 votes at an assembly.

The time comes for the election, the first ballot takes place, and that first announcement of results is always the most exciting, because no one has any idea. 26 candidates receive votes. And there at the top of the list with a substantial lead is me. I immediately refer back to my New Testament Greek.

O, *crapos*.

This is followed by the buzz of the assembly.

Who the heck, is Dana Hanson?

Nice campaign slogan.

There are more ballots taken. I'm still leading but by smaller margins. And now I am the only conservative left.

Then it's time to give a speech. I have a choice, give the speech I wrote, or give the speech that will cater to the voters. Well, most of what I had written was heavily informed by Dallas' thinking. I started out with these words,

"There is an elephant in the middle of the room here. No one wants to talk about it. We are all skirting around it. We want to pretend the elephant isn't here. But, he is. The elephant is this:

We're so busy trying to love our neighbor that we are ignoring loving the Lord God, first. We need to get back to our first love, God, or for some of us here, loving God for the first time. And pastors, this all begins with us.

We are so busy chasing after the latest social cause, that we forget the First Cause. Making disciples. Reaching people for Jesus. We are so busy trying to think outside of the box, that we forgot something else. There is one rectangle I will never step outside of (then I lift up my big Bible)…the Holy Word of God."

It only gets worse from there. If people had garments on, I'm sure they would have rented them. I heard the growing din, and was that gnashing of the teeth?

Well, it came down to me and another candidate and he won. I came in second which shocked everyone, me more than anyone. Friends of mine said the word was, I was "too into the Bible and too into Jesus." Go figure.

Lynn had asked me to call him and tell him the results. So, he was one of the first people I called, and after talking for a bit he said,

"How would you like to meet Dallas?"

This is the summer of 2001. Neither Lynn nor Bill had ever told me they knew Dallas Willard. Know him? Dallas attends their church!

I quickly accept the breakfast invitation, and meet with Lynn and Dallas at Lamplighters Restaurant, on the corner of De Soto and Nordhoff in Chatsworth. This restaurant would prove to be my Capernaum, my Jerusalem, my Harvard, my Oxford, my USC. But, back to the present, we are eating and talking and I finally look across at Dallas and say,

"I ran for bishop of the Lutheran church here and I was shot down in flames! The things I was saying are related to the things I have been learning from your teaching. So, I think you owe it to me to be my mentor."

Dallas chuckled and replied, "I'd be happy."

Thus, began an amazing 12-year journey with my pastor, my spiritual father, my confessor, my friend. Dallas Willard has been an influence in the lives of countless people throughout the world. Many know him more personally than I; all love him dearly.

The mantra is some variation of this:

I have never met anyone who reminds me of what Jesus would be like if he walked the earth today.

Dallas is special to thousands upon thousands of people, but he is uniquely special to me. Do you know why?

While there are many people who knew Dallas Willard in his lifetime, no one in my life, over 57 years, no one other than my wife, Nancy, knows more about me, knows more about what makes me tick, knows more about my weaknesses and challenges, no one knows me as well as Dallas Willard.

That's why you have this book in your hands. We're starting a journey together. I want you to know Father, Son, and Holy Spirit better than ever before, and I can't think of a better way of going about this, then to have the insights of Dallas Willard being used by God to blow away clouds that might be covering your mind.

Think deeply about what you are reading. Go slowly, a day at a time, and you will more and more clearly see the beauty of the Kingdom atmosphere that remains as the breath of the Holy Spirit builds in force and those clouds are lifted.

Join me as your tour guide. I will use what I have learned from Dallas over the years, filtered through what God has been teaching me all along the way, and let the fresh wind blow.

As your tour guide, I am not here to point to me, to highlight my cleverness, or give any astounding insight of Dallas' work, but rather like any good tour guide, I am here to point out the best sights I know.

I am here to give you insight, a little bit each day, but the journey is up to you. Your destination is a transforming life with Jesus. I am here to point to the highlights of his beauty, point to the power of his Kingdom life, and as you open yourself to Jesus and let him work on you, and through you, you will make progress.

I pray you will see these sights in a clearer way, as I did, and you will begin to sense that God has so much more available for you as you live more closely with him.

With Joy on the Journey,

Dana

January 6, 2015

Northridge, CA

1. BEGIN AGAIN

We are designed to be in relationship with Jesus. The Christian life is not a set of rules and regulations. The Bible is not a rulebook, but a description of this way of life. We do not have a list of laws that we follow to become worthy of attention from God. To grow in faith, we live the life we are designed to live, and we are transformed from the inside out.

This is the key. Inside out. Not a flurry of activities that make us acceptable to receive God's love. God already loves us and we are open to being changed from the inside out.

We don't do good things to please God. We become the kind of persons who can do good things naturally because we are being transformed. It is out of the becoming that the doing follows.

What is the most important class you have ever taken? Why was it so key?

Disciples are those seriously intending to become like Jesus from the inside out.
—*Dallas Willard*

2. FACE IT

It's always hilarious when you see a news account of people who look like their dogs. Research on this topic tends to reveal it is not that dogs and their owners (sorry, "caregivers" in LA) grow to resemble each other over time.

It is more likely that the dog owner consciously or unconsciously chooses a pet with similar characteristics. We have a lab/German shepherd mix named, "Nala." She is a sweetheart of a dog, like my sweetheart and wife, Nancy, but when she snarls, she resembles the boys and me.

I do think we take on the appearance of someone over time, however.

Ourselves.

Who we are on the inside begins to reflect more and more on the outside. I remember the story *The Picture of Dorian Gray*, by Oscar Wilde. Dorian is able to live a wild and crazy immoral life without it physically affecting him. Booze, sex, destroying the lives of others—you name it, Dorian did it. Didn't seem to age him a bit. Stayed the same young, good-looking guy. His secret?

He had a portrait of himself that would take in all his sin.

It got uglier and more sinister looking. I won't give away the ending in case you haven't read it, but let's just say Dorian found out the truth.

You begin to notice that about people. Those of us who have been around a while show who we are on the inside by what we look like on the outside. Our faces take on smile lines or frown lines. Anger, like a twisted plastic surgeon, etches pain felt and pain dished out. Botox is no antidote for bile.

So, what do you do? Changing the inside changes the outside. You have a choice in life. There is a God who forgives what's on the inside so you can be transformed into the kind of person who will shine with his glory on the outside. You are more than just your physical body.

Look closely at your own face. Especially around your eyes and the corners of your mouth. What do you see?

You are a spiritual being having a human experience.
—Dallas Willard

3. Seeing is Believing?

There really is no such thing as "science." There are many different fields called "sciences," but there is no theory that wraps them all together. Though there are scientists who make claims for a "theory of everything," no one has come close.

Did you know that about 96% of the universe is composed of two things that astrophysicists label "dark matter" and "dark energy"? We know they are there, but can't see them or directly measure them.

In other words, only about 4% of what most astrophysicists trust exists can be observed and directly measured. The other 96% is assumed based on the evidence of its effect. It appears that the vast majority of existence is considered reality through trust based on evidence.

Trust based on evidence. Does that sound familiar? It should. This is a good definition of faith!

What if God is real? What if God is the creator of all reality? Then if the sciences are considered our ultimate guide to all of existence, we miss out on the very center of life, God himself.

God is not physical, yet God exists. If God exists then

there are dimensions to our lives that may not be physical but are real. If God is real then an education based on the sciences alone would miss out on the most important information of all. Knowledge of God would be absolutely essential. Without studying God, we would be, well, uneducated.

How can we have any knowledge of God if we can't see him?

We don't seem to have trouble claiming knowledge of a lot of stuff we can't see. Like, maybe, 96% of everything?

What are reasons people give for not thinking there is a God? Which argument is the strongest?

Faith is to trust in something to the degree that you are willing to act upon it as if it were true.
—Dallas Willard

4. WON'T-POWER

I am not going to get angry anymore. No, really I'm not. This time I really mean it!

I AM NOT GOING TO GET ANGRY!

Whenever we want to change something about ourselves, the direct approach is usually the way we choose to go. We try willpower. It might as well be won't-power because the direct method almost never works.

We can't convince ourselves to change. For a while it may be possible. Then we come under stress and our changes change back. The harder we try, the more frustrated we get. What is the problem?

The problem is commonly called Self-help. Every Self-help magazine article tells us that we can do it. Go to *Barnes & Noble* and check out the Self-help section.

If you can't lose weight/be friendlier/be more confident in five easy steps, then there must be something wrong with you. After all, the author seems to say, If I did it and wrote a book about it, then you can, too. Not write the book, of course, but you can change.

So, why don't you?

To change from the inside out doesn't last on our own power. We need something more. Recovery groups like AA know this to be true.

They teach that you have to give yourself over to a higher power to be sober. You can't fight unhealthy behavior directly. Alcoholics can stop drinking when they place their trust outside of themselves. This is a great start and if they want to do more than just get sober, they can live a transformed life by opening up to the Holy Spirit.

Jesus designed us and so, naturally, he holds the key to lasting change. Where could you use change in your life right now?

A discipline in any area is something in my power that I do to enable me to do what I cannot do by direct effort.
—Dallas Willard

5. MY ROLE

In 2004, Jamie Foxx won an Oscar for *Ray*. The acting was so good; it's as if he was Ray Charles. You could say, Foxx really sunk into the role.

In the language of the Bible there is a word for this "sinking into." *Enduo*. Romans 13:14 reads,

Rather, clothe yourselves with the Lord Jesus Christ...
(Romans 13:14)

We are to, literally, "sink into" our role as followers of Jesus. This doesn't mean we try to look like him on the outside. Did you know there are still groups of people who wander around in robes and sandals warning about the end of the world?

They think they are supposed to look like Jesus. That's not the point. It's not trying to look like Jesus. Who knows what he looked like anyway? What is important is sinking into the role of being like Jesus on the inside.

To clothe yourself with Jesus is part of the inside/out process. We become like Jesus on the inside so that the things we do on the outside are done as Jesus would do them if he were us in any given situation.

Imagine what Jesus might have looked like.

> *Not WWJD, but what would Jesus do*
> *if he were us in any given situation?*
> —*Dallas Willard*

6. It's All Good

When we declare something good, it doesn't mean it's all good. There is a phrase that has been around for a while that shows this.

It's all good.

The phrase probably originated in rap music and was the slogan of the National Basketball Association for awhile. I am interested who first started saying this because I would like to tell them, it's not all good.

There are people who think of ways to destroy you and they don't even know you. That's not all good. There are people whom you will come to trust who will betray you when you least expect it. That's not all good. What can you do?

When we say "It's all good", though, we know deep down that it's not all good, we say the words like some kind of magical chant in order to convince ourselves that it doesn't matter. Yet, we know it matters.

Perhaps we don't think anyone else cares enough to actually be concerned that it's not all good in our lives. Yet, there is one who does care. It starts with being open and vulnerable to him. How?

We become the kind of people who can care. When Jesus transforms us from the inside out, then we can see things through his eyes for the first time. Then, we don't declare, "It's all good," but we can say with confidence, "There is hope and it starts with Jesus working through me."

What do you need to be completely honest with God about? What is holding you back from opening up all the way to him?

We don't try hard to love someone,
we become the kind of person who can love.
—Dallas Willard

7. Who Am I?

God designs us. We are all wired a certain way. What we have in common you could call:

The essence of our humanity.

The dimensions of our existence.

What makes a person a person?

Jesus gives us an understanding of what our human nature is made of in his answer to a lawyer's question,

What is the most important commandment?

"Love God and neighbor with everything you are."

What are we?

Jesus breaks it down to five parts:

Heart (or Spirit, or Will)

Soul

Mind

Strength (Body)

Neighbor (Social Dimension)

If I can understand what makes me human, then I can begin to see how transformation affects all parts of my life. Let's look at each of these dimensions and their relationship to spiritual formation.

**Think on the word, "dimension."
Expand your thinking on this.**

*The five parts of who we are correspond
with loving God and loving neighbor.*
—*Dallas Willard*

8. HEART

We use the word heart a lot. Even with young children. We often teach little ones to love Jesus with all their heart. We ask them, "Where is Jesus?" They reply, "Jesus is in my heart," as they point to their tummies. I don't teach Jesus this way with small children. I teach them Jesus is all around them covering them everywhere. Yes, he's in your heart, and he is all around you.

Then what about the heart? The biblical understanding of the word, when it is not referring to the actual physical organ in your body, has to do with your choices.

Will, spirit and heart are basically interchangeable words in the Bible. Your heart has to do with the choices you make. Your will and your spirit also have to do with choices. You can substitute the word, "choices," when you see these other words and it will usually be an accurate understanding.

Choice assumes action. To choose is to exercise your own freedom. When you love the Lord God with all your heart, you seek the good of God's plan through your choices. You actively partner with God to bring about what he wants brought about in the life you are leading together. To put your heart into it is to live as if it were so.

What is a choice that you are putting off?

The heart is where we make our choices.
—Dallas Willard

9. SOUL

You are not a collection of specific isolated ingredients. You are a being, united and enmeshed into one unique human. Your soul is the glue that holds your heart, mind, body, and social relations together. Your soul coordinates your life and manages the interaction of the other parts of who you are.

I live my life through my soul. I am hardly conscious of its work. The soul is not physical, but it is real. It is hard to understand the awesome nature of my soul, and of the five parts of who I am, it is the most involved. The soul responds to all aspects of my life.

God desires to transform my soul. It is not holy and pure on its own, but needs changing like all the other parts of who I am. If I want to be like Jesus, I need to be transformed from the very depths of who I am.

Look at this vision to transform your soul. This is the most challenging aspect of who you are, at least to explain, but it is essential that you understand. You have to have the "big picture" view of everything else.

What has been your understanding of the word, "soul"?

Our soul is the glue that holds your heart, mind, body, and social relations together.

—Dallas Willard

10. Mind: Thinking

"Love the Lord your God with all of your mind…"

The mind is separated from the heart, but it works with it. The mind is constantly providing direction for the choices we make. The mind is further divided into two parts. Thoughts and feelings.

Thinking is where we process the world around us. We can consider many things in relationship to other things. Thinking is where we have the capacity to use imagination. It is where we form opinions and perceptions which we may or may not act upon. In a healthy mind, we use a set of standards called, "logic," which help us measure our thoughts.

Our thinking is influenced by our feeling. It is our emotional response to what is being processed. Something may be logical, but we may feel that it is wrong. Two people can think in an identical way about something, but have a very different response because of how they feel. We are often pulled away from right thinking because we allow how we feel to take priority. This is where we can get into big trouble.

When is a time when you went with your feelings instead of what seemed most logical and it worked out? How about a time it was the wrong decision?

The mind is divided into thoughts and feelings.
—Dallas Willard

11. MIND: FEELINGS

Feelings follow after the thinking the mind is doing. Feelings can become a priority once our minds are convinced that we are in charge.

If only everyone would think like us.

If it is our desires that matter the most, then feelings can bring plenty of destruction.

When our feelings clash with our thinking, the effect can be dangerous. Like the effect of the ring on Gollum in the *Lord of the Rings*,

"Whatever we wants, precious, that's whats we try to get."

The emotional pull of possessing what we want makes it impossible to care about the needs of anyone else. Then obsession can take over.

Take dating, for instance. As long as I am having my needs met by you, I am in love with you. How quickly that changes when you don't do what I want or I am not getting the attention I feel I deserve.

Conflict quickly moves in, and with me at the center of the universe, obviously, you must be wrong. Either you change your act immediately, or I am out of here. I'll simply fall in love with someone else until my needs aren't being met again. Follow your desires? There are many times that is the last thing you should possibly do.

What is one thing in your life that has more to do with following your desires than doing the right thing?

Our feelings can be a good servant but they are a terrible master.
—Dallas Willard

12. BODY

When we turn from God's ways, our bodies become a popular place where sin is lived out. Self-worship can deal directly with our looks and how we physically feel. This can bring us pseudo-joy.

That is why no one is really interested in how Hollywood stars are thinking lately. Yet, you scroll through any entertainment website and you will see examples like:

"10 best beach bodies in Hollywood"

"10 worst celebrity plastic surgery disasters"

On occasion, I read Cracked or TMZ online, or US and People magazines, and I am always amazed at how much emphasis is on what stars look like. Most of these artists are actors and singers, not models.

I realize that thin is still in, and yes, Matthew McConaughey does have an excellent six pack, even for a man his age. Better than my one pack. But what about their skills and what they have to teach us about their art?

Then there is the obsession with sexual feelings as it relates to my body. With advertisers, I am often invited to try any product with the understanding that I am going to be sexually satisfied, or more sexually satisfied as a result. Most products out there are marketed with some nod to sexuality. Our God-given creativity and imagination seem to be stuck in connecting everything to sex.

Obviously, alcohol, other mind enhancing/altering drugs, pornography, and violence are mainstays for entertainment. More than anything, they are about the body. We are bombarded with a message of feel good, or a message of don't feel at all.

Before good spam blockers came along, we were constantly bombarded with the two "V's": Viagra and Vicodin.

Viagra and Vicodin are not what I need.

Making bad choices with my body is not what I need.

What I need is freedom.

When is the last time you looked in a full-length mirror? What did you see?

The least understood aspect of progress in Christlikeness is the role of the body in the spiritual life.
— Dallas Willard

13. Social Relations

Love your neighbor as yourself.

This is the social relationship part of who we are. God created us as social beings. This is one of the key parts of being created in the image of God. Being able to relate to one another and God. God himself relates to himself as a social being in the Trinity. This is mind boggling…

God living with God's self in the existence of Father, Son, and Holy Spirit chooses to invite us into the love and joy of this Trinitarian reality.

How is that for big words? In other words, Father, Son and Holy Spirit are having such a good time living for the sake of each other that God decides, "Let's create people to share in the joy!"

We are born to party!

Well…something like that. You live out who you are in the community of who you are with. A vital part of what makes you who you are is me and a vital part of what makes me is you.

Think of a lonely time in your life. What was it like?

We are invited to live in Trinitarian reality.
— Dallas Willard

14. FREEDOM

The story of humanity is one people group joining together to survive with another. Whether family or loosely organized social arrangements of another kind, it is about gaining enough power to resist others who want that power. Whether by conquest or treaty, no one lives in a place where someone else has not lived before. Family, tribe or nation, the human story is one of conquest and compromise for survival.

In a way then, no one is born free. We are beholden to others in order to survive. This begins in immediate family, to be sure, but the continued dependence we have on each other makes the idea of a self-made man or woman, meaningless.

We are not free, but dependent. We will either learn to work together, or we manipulate and overpower in order to work together to get what we want. Cooperation or exploitation become the human response. Then what is freedom? How can I be free if I am connected to others in a positive or negative way?

This is freedom. Freedom is the ability to discern what is good for me and good for others, and do it. By my own human nature, I cannot consistently live my life for the sake of others. By God's power, I can.

So, the only true freedom is to know what is good for me and others, and, through the guidance and power of the Holy Spirit, be able to do it.

We are free to live for each other. Free to serve. Free to give privilege a rest. Through Jesus, we celebrate our own independence from being dependent on our human nature.

What does it mean to know you may be a slave to what you want, but free to live for the sake of others?

Freedom is to consistently want the good and be able to do it.
— Dallas Willard

15. Living Freedom

To live out true freedom, we need God. When we live out our lives based on our human nature, we end up being vulnerable to deceiving ourselves. We have no benchmark for comparison. Like a compass without true north.

Here is when what is not good is called good. Seeking the truth is intolerance. Disagreeing with someone is hate. Life without God is chaotic.

It doesn't have to be this way. I don't have to do what my thoughts, feelings, body, social pressures, and even my very soul itself, tell me to do. There is freedom to choose. God can take action in my choices.

Left alone without God's influence, my heart can't handle the pressure. Then there are times I will do the things I know are wrong and not do the things I know are right. Life without God is life ruled by me.

Honestly, I can't trust myself to have my own best interest at heart. My choices may be ruled by my desires rather than by God's desires. I will not even acknowledge that I am not doing right. All my parts will find a way to convince me that I am OK. I will hear the truth defined by me, and not by God. This is what I sound like:

>Go with your instincts.
>You deserve it.
>Everyone else is doing it.
>You're only human.
>You were born this way.
>Life without God is dangerous because it seems so natural.
>There is another way.

Who are the morally conservative atheist thinkers popular in our society today? Trick question?

>*Life without God is life ruled by me.*
>*— Dallas Willard*

16. Life with God

A life moving toward God, rather than centered on yourself, becomes a possibility when your heart aligns with God's desires. When our choices are the choices God would make for us, we begin transformation. All the other parts of our lives are affected. Soul, mind, body, and social relations are all involved in the process.

Here is what is different about a renovation of the heart. It is not simply trying harder or getting more focused on the choices we make. It is not a direct approach at all. Remember willpower? It cannot be sustained. Every part of you will scream out, "It can't be done!"

Life with God is different. There is no part of you that cannot be transformed under the power of the Holy Spirit. Jesus is our model. We learn from Jesus how to live life as he would live it if he were us in any given situation. This begins with understanding what life is like without God.

Are you moving toward God or away from God?
Think on this.

We learn from Jesus how to live life as he would live it if he were us in any given situation.
— *Dallas Willard*

17. Radical Ruin

We make good choices. We make disastrous choices. Why the difference? It really has to do with who we are and the paths we choose.

There are basically two paths. The first path is the one we start out on and most of us stay on. This is the self-worship path. Or, the path to radical ruin.

Self-worship means we put ourselves and our desires on the throne of our lives. We are the center of the universe.

It is like when we are one year old and we can't distinguish between ourselves and the world around us. In some ways, for most of us, this never changes. We grow older but we don't grow up. Until Jesus is on the throne of our lives, radical ruin is the outcome waiting for us in any possible given situation. John Maxwell says it this way,

"Unless God is in control of your life; your life is out of control."

Our human nature is to focus on ourselves and what we want. The mantra of a normal person is this:

I want what I want when I want it.

Any alternatives? One.

The second path is that of self-denial. This doesn't mean we deny who we are and the condition we are in, rather it means we choose not to give in to our normal desires, which are to seek pleasure and be in control. Self-denial is the path to radical goodness. Where we live for the sake of others.

Self-denial doesn't demean us. This doesn't turn us into doormats to be stepped on or be taken advantage of. Self-denial enhances who we are and puts us on the path of God's design. When Jesus is on the throne of our lives, we are finally our best, true selves. How does this happen?

It has to do with the five parts of who we are again: heart, mind, soul, body, and social life.

Radical ruin or radical goodness?

Time to choose.

This cannot be done for us, but under the influence of God's grace, it is possible to choose goodness.

Think of times when you denied something that you wanted and it actually worked out better?

Grace is not opposed to effort. It is opposed to earning.
— Dallas Willard

18. RUINED HEART

"Acting on belief as if it were so" is a good definition of faith. When an atheist claims there is no God, that belief may not be based on a solid body of evidence; rather a lack of evidence. It is a readiness to act as if certain things were not so. Even going against what we see and experience around us.

> *Romans 1:20 (NLT)*
> *From the time the world was created, people have seen the earth and sky and all that God made. They can clearly see his invisible qualities—his eternal power and divine nature. So they have no excuse whatsoever for not knowing God.*

Today, we are able to see way more of "earth and sky and all that God made." The evidence for design in the universe, the big bang evidence for space, time, energy and matter being created simultaneously, all of these point to a likely conclusion that there is a causative, extra-dimensional agency. This doesn't specifically warrant this being the God of the Bible, but there is other evidence for that being the case. Let's just consider a "god" in general.

Why do a small minority of people not trust there is a god? Why do many more people act as if there is no god?

I think the challenge is, if God exists then God must somehow be in charge. If God is in charge then guess what? I'm not.

The path of ruin begins with the heart. Choices are made as if there is no god. These choices affect all the other parts of our lives. We wish to be in charge and if God does exist we can't logically hold on to that viewpoint. So we begin to deceive ourselves in one of two ways. We either choose to believe there is no God, or we act as if there is no God. Either way we lose.

This is why unhealthy behavior by atheists and by people who identify as Christian looks very similar. One ignores the consequences of there being a God, and the other acts as if God doesn't care. If we keep choosing to ignore God, we also ignore the blessings God has for us. When our hearts are turned in another direction, we cannot be our best, true selves we are created to be.

Look for evidence of God today.

Disbelief, not unbelief is what an atheist experiences. It is a readiness to act as if certain things were not so.
— Dallas Willard

19. Ruined Mind

When we choose not to deal with God, then our minds have to go to work. We need to find ways to convince ourselves that God doesn't exist or God doesn't matter.

We have worked on this in our country with some interesting mental gymnastics. In the public square, we attempt to follow a strict Darwinian evolution model, for example, and desperately hold on to natural selection and random mutation as the sole mechanisms for the development of life. However, a strict interpretation of this position is becoming more and more difficult to defend.

Origins of life research ("abiogenesis") provides an impossible scenario for a strict view of Darwinian evolution. In order for natural selection and random mutation to occur in the first place, you need something to select from. Something to mutate. The apparent necessity of an outside agent of some kind getting the ball rolling is simply dismissed as something beyond the scope of discussion.

Those who do believe in God may also be tempted to follow viewpoints that may be more about themselves than about God's desire, focusing on what they want, not what God wants.

One of the interesting attempts to cloud our thinking about God today is to is question the validity of God's Word. When a Bible scholar goes out of their way to try to show the Bible doesn't really mean what it says it means, there needs to be evidence to the contrary that has been rationally tested.

Some scholars choose to say the teachings of the Bible are outdated or not relevant. They say the Bible writers couldn't comprehend our issues of complexity.

The challenge of taking this position on the Bible is that it places a person outside of the scope of traditional Christianity. Christians claim God is the source of the Bible. So, God is certainly capable of knowing about situations we face in life today, and inspiring Bible writers to address them in a general way.

Once our choices turn us away from God, then our thinking goes to work. Deceiving ourselves in order to get what we want is not a difficult task. We are experts at it. Self-worship and deception are a great match.

What are some other issues upheld by traditional Christian morality that are being challenged today?

An unreasonable person refuses to test
or consider criticisms of his beliefs.
— Dallas Willard

20. Ruined Relationships

As we experience mind ruin and the emotional ruin that goes along with it, our interaction with other people is never really authentically beneficial. I liken it to a dance where we try to move each other around the dance floor. If both partners are trying to lead at the same time it doesn't work.

Social ruin is seen in the lack of depth in our friendships. It is seen in the struggles of marriage. It is a key source of the dissatisfaction so many have with their jobs. If I am trying to remain in charge of my life, when things don't go my way, I will usually respond in one of two ways:

Neurosis or character disorder.

Author M. Scott Peck considers these two responses in his classic work, *The Road Less Traveled*. When I am struggling in life, I place the blame on myself or others in an exaggerated way. When I am always wrong, it is neurosis. When someone else is always wrong it is character disorder. Here is how it works.

For a neurotic person, I try to remain in control by putting huge demands of perfection upon myself, coupled with low expectations. In this way when someone fails me, I can always blame it on me. I stay in control because life is happening just like I predicted. Eeyore, from Winnie the Pooh, is an example of this neurotic response.

For a character disorder person, I try to remain in control by placing the blame for anything that goes wrong in my life squarely where it belongs. On you. Or anyone else. On the government. On multi-national corporations. On society in general. Blame it on the man.

Never, in any waking moment, would my problems be owned up to as my problems. In character disorder, I am always the victim. After all, if I am the center of my own universe, how can any conflict, failure or disappointment be my doing?

In our relationships, then, we may operate out of neurosis or character disorder, and usually it is a combination, but the results are the same. A life going against our own design.

Do you function more with neurosis or character disorder?

The world is not going to end if I don't get my own way.
— Dallas Willard

21. Ruined Body

When our choices work against the health of our body, deception moves in. Take food for instance.

When it comes to food it seems everything that is not healthy for you is also what you like the most. Salt, sugar and fat are great at giving temporary pleasure and yes, even comfort.

I like donuts as much as Homer Simpson. I like donuts too much. I never met a donut I didn't like. Long johns, custard-filled, cake, powdered, sprinkled, and any kind of cruller. Chocolate-covered crullers, maple-covered crullers, plain crullers, pretty much the whole cruller family…You get the idea.

And it's not just donuts. Don't get me started on pizza…

You see, I am very skilled at wanting to eat in abundance that which I should be eating in moderation. I am an expert at eating what is unhealthy. This is no problem for me. I have never had to find a program to get me to eat donuts and pizza.

That's what radical ruin is like. What is unhealthy is easy to accomplish. We are experts at denial and manipulation. No one has to teach us these kinds of things.

It is fascinating to listen to people suddenly speak in sophisticated terms when they are trying to explain something they know just isn't right. We are natural experts at fooling ourselves and we deceive ourselves into thinking we are fooling others. Certainly not always the case.

Denial, deception, and manipulation are all characteristics of self-worship. We become outstanding negotiators of convincing ourselves that what is plainly and completely wrong—isn't.

Jesus summed it up like this:

> *Matthew 16:26 (NLT)*
> *And how do you benefit if you gain the whole world but lose your own soul in the process? Is anything worth more than your soul?*

Where have you been trying to fool yourself lately?

When we are fasting it is God fasting with us and through us.
— Dallas Willard

22. RUINED SOUL

Self-worship affects every part of us. The final impact is on everything we are. The soul, that holds it all together, is in ruin. When we mistake ourselves for God, then God becomes meaningless or an enemy. We cannot want him. If we work against God in every part our being, we become the kind of people who cannot want God.

Jesus speaks about hell often. "Hell" is to be separated from the presence of God forever. When you have soul ruin, hell is a possible destination. It is not so much God sends people to hell. Hell is a choice. If you constantly don't want God in your life, eventually you become the kind of person who can't want God in your life.

God gives us the freedom to make our own choice when it comes to living with him. If we choose to separate from God, he reluctantly allows this because to force us to live with him goes against his nature. God is love.

Often people will speak of death-bed conversions where someone denies God all their life, and before they die, they repent and seek him. Is this authentic?

Well, that person may have been seeking all along and it

just finally surfaced in the light of day, or they finally publicly acknowledged this, so, yes, I think it is possible.

Yet, is it probable? Not likely. If life away from God is the life we are choosing to live, then, eventually, being with God may not be an option that is within our realm of choice. God has an infinitely flexible will; we do not. No one "just misses out" of heaven. Life without God is a constant choice that keeps a person focused in a radical ruin direction. In the end, God is faithful to our choices.

To paraphrase a thought from C.S. Lewis,

"Instead of one who trusts saying, 'Thy will be done,' God says to the person in soul ruin, 'Thy will be done.'"

When it comes to sharing the Gospel, spending so much time and energy on those who don't want God only results in less time and energy reaching out to those who do want him, but just don't know him, yet. Do you agree with this? Think of why or why not.

Hell is the best God can do for some people.
— Dallas Willard

23. RUIN IS EASY

The path to radical ruin is wide and easy. It is made possible by following our own desires.

It looks like this:

- Make choices based on your interests.
- Do what you think best.
- Do whatever your gut instinct tells you to do.
- Do whatever makes you feel good.
- Don't worry about how you affect someone else.
- Don't think about the consequences of anything.
- Just do it.

This is the life of radical ruin. It looks strangely like the normal life of an animal. Yes, we are animals, but we have been created in God's image which includes the ability to choose. There is another path we can choose. The path to radical goodness.

Here is the choice. Either you choose a life apart from God or a life set apart by God. This is the meaning of the word "holy." To be set apart.

The way to holy living begins and ends with self-denial. This is the antidote to self-worship. Again, this doesn't mean self-rejection. It is not designed to take away our dignity so we can become doormats; allowing everyone to step all over us.

Self-denial is dying to having to be the center of the universe and allowing Jesus to rule on the throne of our lives. Death to self brings life in Christ. The ultimate reference point in our lives becomes God. We live according to what he wants rather than what we want.

Living with Jesus on the throne of your life, where he lives for you and through you, brings about a restoration of your very soul. You can do what he wants rather than what you want. You can become the kind of person who lives in his Kingdom now as he desires you to live. As the words of the ancient psalm proclaim,

Psalm 23:3 (KJV)
He restoreth my soul: he leadeth me in the paths of righteousness for his name's sake.

The answer to the "What is the meaning of life?" question is...

The cost of discipleship is nothing compared to the cost of non-discipleship.
— Dallas Willard

24. Our Purpose

What is the central focus of our lives as we are following Jesus?

God and neighbor.

Loving God and loving our neighbor becomes the key. We are created with love of God and neighbor as our purpose. When we think of the deep questions of human life, this is how we are designed.

What is the meaning of life?

What is my purpose?

Loving God and loving your neighbor.

The bestselling classic book *The Purpose Driven Life*, by Rick Warren, needs only one paragraph to answer the purpose question. The purpose of every single human being is identical. "Love God and neighbor." The differences all revolve around the question, "How?"

The life of radical goodness is to give and forgive. Give of yourself for the sake of the other, seek forgiveness when you mess up, and forgive when you are wronged. But, if we are always giving and forgiving doesn't that mean our lives become all about losing and sacrifice? In the God and neighbor centered-life it is just the opposite. As we reach out, we are enhanced and expanded. Jesus said it this way,

> *Luke 6:37-38 (NLT)*
> *"Stop judging others, and you will not be judged. Stop criticizing others, or it will all come back on you. If you forgive others, you will be forgiven. If you give, you will receive. Your gift will return to you in full measure, pressed down, shaken together to make room for more, and running over. Whatever measure you use in giving—large or small—it will be used to measure what is given back to you."*

The path of self-denial is possible because that is how we are designed by God. We are perfectly safe to let God worry about our desires and needs. We don't have to try to enhance our own lives by constantly looking out for #1.

God is always looking out for us.

We are free to give everything we have, and everything we are, to God and neighbor. Our very soul is given back to us and we become truly human for the very first time. This is just what God has in mind all along.

What does loving God look like to you?

> *We are perfectly safe to let God worry about our desires and needs.*
> *— Dallas Willard*

25. A Picture

Our love of God directly impacts our love of neighbor. When we truly receive God's love, it becomes possible to love our neighbor. Not for what I can get out of my neighbor, but out of genuine generosity. Through this process, the five parts of who I am (heart, soul, mind, body, social relations) come into proper alignment. More and more, I am living as I am designed to live.

The choices I make out of my heart are for the benefit of others.

My soul is in harmony with God's intentions.

My mind is filled with thoughts and feelings that focus on good rather than tempt me toward evil.

My body is used to worship and glorify God rather than pursue pleasure and power.

All of this affects the people in my life.

As I am dying to myself, it is not all about me. I am becoming the kind of person who does not have a crisis when I don't get my own way. It does not surprise me or bother me. I am confident that I am perfectly safe in God's hands and will face life centered within his presence.

As I become a student of Jesus and his ways, I am able to live in his Kingdom now. Instead of feeling I belong away from God and becoming more and more a person who cannot want him, by dying to myself, I am at home with Jesus and living my life as he would lead it if he were me. This is a reality waiting to be discovered.

Changing from the inside out is possible and it is the only option for true living. Then I will live as I have been designed to live all along, and I will be at home with Jesus. I will be my best, true self.

When do you support an unhealthy life being lived out by a friend?

It does not surprise me or bother me
when I don't get my own way.
— Dallas Willard

26. PARTNERS

In order to have lasting transformation, Jesus chooses to partner with us. Without Jesus I can do nothing, but if I do nothing, it will certainly be without Jesus.

The path of self-denial is a one of cooperation. Not everyone understands this. I come out of a Lutheran faith tradition. One of our theological challenges is we so strongly emphasize grace and God's work in our lives that we end up warping the biblical picture of God working with us. Here are some results:

- When we respond to our salvation by doing good works, our efforts are seen as "works righteousness".
- We are trying to earn God's love if we talk about doing the right things.
- The spiritual disciplines are not a focal point of life because they are human effort to earn God's favor.

It's as if, after we become Christian, we are supposed to just sit back and be transformed through some kind of spiritual osmosis.

That is not the reality of Kingdom life, however.

By fearing we would have a heart attack if we dare speak of doing something to grow in our faith, we become complacent in our non-response. Strangely, for some Christians, it becomes a badge of honor not to do anything.

Transformation doesn't happen this way. This is why the lives of most Christians don't differ that much from anyone else. Without partnering with Jesus, we are on our own. He will not do our self-denial for us. It's not about sitting around and waiting to die or have Jesus return someday, whichever comes first. Jesus actually wants to work with us in his Kingdom now.

Yes, there is another way.

You can call it VIM. Effort falls into the category of VIM. This is an acronym for Vision, Intention, and Means. Through this three-step process, Jesus transforms us into the kind of people who can do the things he would do if he were us in any situation.

Next, what does VIM look like?

"We don't do good things so that God loves us. God loves us, and our response of thanksgiving is to do good things." Explain.

> *Without Jesus I can do nothing, but if I do nothing,*
> *it will certainly be without Jesus.*
> *— Dallas Willard*

27. VISION

We start with a vision to be a Kingdom person. This is someone who is actively working with God in bringing blessing, love and joy into the world. Before we can understand this we need to define "Kingdom."

Kingdom of God—the range of God's effective will

We have confidence that God's will is done everywhere. Therefore, his Kingdom is infinite because his domain is wherever there is the possibility his choices are accomplished. We pray this frequently.

Thy Kingdom come: Thy Will be done: On earth as it is in heaven.

This is our possible life. Where God's desires and our destiny are identical. We are invited to the greatest cause of the galaxies. To live our lives the way we are designed to live. It's like this.

Everyone in the world may be working against God's Kingdom coming because they have given in to a life of self-worship. Yet, if we are working for the sake of God and others, as we are being transformed, creation itself is being transformed because we have chosen to follow God's Kingdom vision.

How could we live in any safer, richer, more joyful place than in the reality of what God wants done? Do you think he can accomplish what he intends to accomplish?

Then you have vision.

What do you really want?

> *The key to loving God is to see Jesus.*
> — *Dallas Willard*

28. INTENTION

Here is where we start to get bogged down when it comes to spiritual growth. Two things happen.

1. We say we want to grow, but we don't really trust we can.
2. We don't really intend to obey what we learn in the first place.

Intention is about thinking it through.

There is a whole area of study that is critical to trusting in Jesus.

Apologetics, which includes:

- Making a case for Christ.
- Defending my faith.
- Articulating why I believe what I believe.

In Christian apologetics, you make a logical case for your faith in Jesus. You build confidence in the reasonability of the Christian faith. Why is it important to trust intellectually?

You cannot sustain a living, influential faith in Jesus unless you trust in what he says and does. Apologetics would say you cannot thrive as a follower of Jesus unless you have confidence that:

- The Bible is the Word of God.
- Jesus is who he says he is.
- The Christian worldview is the most reasonable and rational view of reality of all religions and philosophies.

A simple faith learned in Sunday School does not survive teenage and adult skepticism in a person who is truly testing out their faith. You can get by with "Jesus loves me" when times are good, but when crisis and uncertainty hit, which they will, to have confidence in the authenticity of your experience and the evidence of the truth of the Gospel are essential.

The good news is: Jesus is totally trustworthy, and so we can follow his ways.

Christians are not really honest on this point. Often we talk a good faith but we don't live it. Usually, this has something to do with focusing almost entirely on a God of love and forgiveness.

Yet, God is also a God of justice and right living. The God who totally loves us is the God who totally expects obedience. We emphasize all the accounts in the Bible where Jesus is caring and forgiving, but many times we skip over his call for radical self-denial.

For example, when he tells the woman who is caught in adultery, "*Go, and sin no more,*" he wasn't winking at her when he said it (John 8:1-11).

We can choose not to sin.

We can choose to do what is right.

It is possible to do this in this life. We are already a new creation when we place our trust in Jesus and begin to live in his Kingdom now. A new species. We do not have to give in to our old human desires for pleasure and power.

The fact that we fail at times, and fall back into our sinful human ways, doesn't cancel out the equally truthful fact that with the Holy Spirit working through us we can choose not to sin. Unless we go into this whole enterprise intending to live a transformed life, we will fail before we get started.

We can live our lives as Jesus would live our lives if he were us. But, we must want to do this.

What do you really want?

You can't say you trust in Christ and not intend to obey him.
— Dallas Willard

29. MEANS

The way to live in God's Kingdom now is to work around every part of our normal self so we trust that we can actually be transformed. This is an indirect approach. If you take the direct approach it is bound to fail. Trying to use your will to convince yourself. Take patience, for instance.

This time I am really going to live a godly life! I am going to quit being so impatient. I am going to be patient and I am going do it—right now!

Whenever we take the direct approach, it seems our human nature instantly cries out,

It can't be done!

Or,

Who do you think you are?!

Or,

I'll just die if I follow through on this!

Transformation uses an indirect approach. The spiritual disciplines that Jesus practiced are the key.

Through things like silence and solitude, study, worship and prayer, we are able to focus on what is there in front of us, and it will naturally be used by the Spirit to change us from the inside. We practice living things we can in order to have changed the things we can't.

For instance, we don't say,

From now on I am going to be a loving person.

Rather we say,

I am going to work on becoming the kind of person who can freely love others.

The spiritual disciplines then become tools that make us available for transformation and become that person.

Think about the various types of self-help you have attempted. What were some challenges?

We practice living things we can do
in order to have changed the things we can't do.
— Dallas Willard

30. AN EXAMPLE

To understand the VIM process, let's look at weight loss.

For most adults in America, one area we frequently wish to change is being overweight. If you take all the weight loss products, all the weight loss programs, all the health club memberships, and all the diet books, then you add it all together, you are looking at billions of billions of dollars.

Yet, most people simply go through a cycle of losing and gaining. Most people don't see permanent results. Why? There are many psychological and physiological factors, but many times it may be a matter of VIM. Could it be with weight loss we go directly to means, without really addressing vision and intention? Here is what VIM might look like.

Vision for weight loss

Think about what you would look like if you lost weight. Would you be more attractive? The bit of narcissism in all of us would enjoy that. Think about what it would feel like if you didn't have to carry around those extra pounds every day. The aches and pains in your joints. Just the overall dragging that goes on by the end of the day. Wouldn't it be wonderful to face the world as John Winger (Bill Murray) proclaims in the film, *Stripes*:

You are a lean, mean, fighting machine!

Do you have a vision for weight loss?

Intention for weight loss

Vision is not enough. You can't just sit there daydreaming about how great it would be to lose weight. You can't just read testimonials. You have to carefully consider what life would be like as a slimmer you. You have to count the cost. Jesus knows that.

> *Luke 14:28 (NLT)*
> *But don't begin until you count the cost. For who would begin construction of a building without first getting estimates and then checking to see if there is enough money to pay the bills?*

After this careful consideration, if you are truly ready this time, then you state you intentions. Maybe you confide in a friend that this time you really mean it. You have a vision for weight loss. You have the intention to do what it takes to achieve it. Now, the final step is the easiest. How to do it. The means.

Means for Weight Loss

Obesity is many times spiritual at its core. David Housolder, in *Light Your Church on Fire Without Burning It Down*, has this to say,

One only has to think of our grossly overweight society, and the massive trillions spent on resulting medical care trying to cure the

symptoms caused by obesity, when there is deep inner pain trying to get covered by overeating. Why not go right to the cause?

Healing prayer can deliver a person from this inner pain. Along with this, healthy habits follow. Proper diet, exercise, and sleep are important for weight loss. A healthy lifestyle includes these three.

Healing prayer and healthy habits are the means to losing what we are dragging through life.

You can see what practicing vision, intention, and means can do for weight loss. What would it look like to change a whole life? Through VIM, you yield yourself to the power of the Holy Spirit for lasting transformation.

Where do you need healing?

> *In the spiritual life it is true that*
> *where there is a will there is a way.*
> — *Dallas Willard*

31. ALL IN

How can we have radical transformation through the five aspects of who we are?

We take steps to change what keeps us from becoming like Jesus. We have the capability of doing this as we partner with Jesus. We begin transforming on the inside, so we might be like Jesus on the outside.

If we go step by step in each of the five areas in detail, what would this process look like when we address something that is getting in the way? Consider anger.

My Heart

I may have grown up in a family where anger is normal and having a bad temper is expected.

My Soul

In all the parts of my being I just keep focusing on my rightness and everyone else's wrongness. I am like a god of my own universe, and I am looking for every opportunity to lash out in wrath at those who would question my goodness.

My Mind

I find reasons why I should be angry about the situation. I make sure I keep focusing on why I have been wronged.

My Social Relations

I look for ways I can always have the upper hand with my friends and family members so I am the one who gets to lash out at them when the opportunity arises. I try to place them in anxiety-producing situations where they are never really comfortable around me.

My Body

Frowning and scowling are my normal facial characteristics and there is nothing so "good" as to raise my voice or whisper in a bitter tone. I enjoy the rush of emotion that attaches to my anger. It makes me feel so alive. I find ways to get the adrenaline flowing and take on a nice red complexion.

Whew! Glad I got that over with!

Where has anger creeped up on you lately?

We are called to lead for God right where we are.
— Dallas Willard

32. BEGIN WITH THE MIND

The first place we move toward a change of heart is through our thoughts. The devil works through our thinking more than anywhere else. Both good thinking or bad thinking are real possibilities because God gives us the freedom to choose our thoughts.

We can't control what is in the world, but we can control what is in our own thoughts. We choose the content of our thinking. We won't always do this perfectly, but we can make progress in filling our minds more and more with God's Word and the promises announced there.

Our thinking is broken down into four parts: Ideas, images, information and intelligence.

Ideas

We have been forming an idea system since we were born. We have been influenced through experience, the teachings of others, and watching the behavior of our family and community. We don't always realize what is reality and what is an illusion in our lives. When we look at our ideas, we do a reality check.

To transform our personal idea system from one of ruin to one of goodness, we have to replace the ideas we hold with the idea system of Jesus. This is the most difficult and painful process we can go through in life. To actually change our minds.

Most people have ideas firmly established when it comes to life's values and beliefs by the time they are about 12-13 years old. At a deep level it is extraordinarily rare for us to change our thinking after that. It is essential that we do so, however, if we want our thinking to be more and more like the thinking of Jesus.

There are many examples of thinking that are destructive in our lives. Consider relativism.

Relativism is the belief that one person's moral ideas have equal value to another person's moral ideas. There is no right or wrong; only what you think is right and wrong. Your ideas are valid if you sincerely follow them. Relativism has a strong influence in our present society. No values can be wrong except, of course, if you disagree with me. Then you are wrong.

Images

Along with ideas, images fill our minds. They are basic and concrete and they have a powerful effect. Ideas and images are the devils main tools against us. What preoccupies our thought life? Ideas and specific images.

Sexual images are overwhelming in society. We see sexualized images in advertisement and the media everywhere. Pleasure and power await us as we think of these images. The multibillion-dollar pornography business is a huge tool that Satan uses today to tie minds to an endless cycle of lust, pleasure, guilt and emptiness.

Jesus uses images to to move us to his way. The most powerful image in this is the cross. To look at a cross is to sense his love, sacrifice, devotion and strength. The cross is a reminder of what he did, but it is also a beacon of hope of what he is doing.

As we are being transformed to be like Jesus, the key is to take the destructive ideas and images we have and replace them with the ideas and images Jesus possesses. We take on the mind of Christ. This is a possibility for life in his Kingdom now.

> *1 Cor. 2:16 (NLT)*
> *"Who can know what the Lord is thinking? Who can give him counsel?"*

But we can understand these things, for we have the mind of Christ.

What are some ideas you have that God might be challenging?

The key to loving God is to see Jesus in your mind
and hold him there clearly.
— Dallas Willard

33. MORE THINKING

Information

1 Thessalonians 5:19-21 (NLT)
Do not stifle the Holy Spirit. Do not scoff at prophe-
cies, but test everything that is said. Hold on to what
is good.

Jesus encourages us to put him to the test. The Christian faith is based on our ability to examine the evidence. We are expected to seek the information that is available to decide for ourselves. The Spirit guides this process, but we are to take the initiative.

Putting the Christian worldview to the test and comparing it to other religions and philosophies is encouraged. Christian schools, colleges and universities have historically been centers of learning to compare and contrast competing worldviews in the search for the truth. Some still are.

Another way God passes on information is a rather unique quality of the Christian faith. It is so culturally transferable.

According to Wycliffe Translators, as of 2013, portions of

the Bible have been translated into over 2,787 languages. This includes 513 languages with complete Bible translations.

This is a strong mark of the "God-breathed" aspect of the Bible's writing, that all cultures in every age are invited to read God's Word for themselves and examine the evidence. It's as if God is saying,

The information is there. Have at it.

Now, compare this to a religion like Islam, where the holy book, the Qu'ran, is only truly considered the Word of Allah if it is in Arabic. There is no movement to compare and contrast what the Quran teaches as relates to other faiths and philosophies. In fact, in some countries where Islamic law reigns, Bibles are not even allowed to be examined, and it can be a crime to talk about the Christian faith.

There are also religions that have secret books written in obscure ways, which only the most enlightened are allowed to read. The God of the Bible wants people to understand. Seeking the truth of Jesus is an active pursuit.

Intelligence

Reason is a gift from God. As we examine the information available in his Word and in the world around us, we have the capability of understanding for ourselves that the Christian worldview is the most reasonable view of reality available.

God doesn't demand our allegiance through blind faith. "Because he said so," is not a Christian teaching.

God invites us into relationship, and God creates us in his image so we have the ability to relate. He invites us to use the intelligence he gives us to begin thinking how bad ideas and images can be replaced by the truth of Jesus.

What would be helpful for you to study as it relates to Jesus?

Christianity is a superior view of reality.
— *Dallas Willard*

34. Changing Thinking

You have the vision to transform your mind. Next comes intention. The fact that you are reading this, is intention enough for me, so I will continue. How do you give access to the Holy Spirit to transform your thought-life?

The Word of God

Memorizing Bible passages is a practice that was simply a necessity for thousands of years. No books.

When writing does come along, it is still so rare and expensive that most people had to continue to memorize. In fact, most of the priests of Israel and the leaders of the early church memorized the whole Bible!

For us, memorizing and letting the Word marinate in our minds, is a strong defense against the ideas and images that would lead us down the wrong path. Passages like Psalm 23 or Colossians 3:1-17, for example, are good scrub brushes for our minds. They leave a shine.

How do I memorize?

There are many examples. Here's one.

Read a section of the Bible, let it sit, read it again, think about it, recite it aloud, think about a word or thought the verses bring to mind, read it again…A similar tool to this has been used for centuries: *Lectio Divini*.

Sound

Another way to fill your mind with God's Word is listening to music and singing. A praise song or hymn, an encouraging or contemplative popular song on the radio, these all can be ways to memorize scripture and God's ways and keep them before your mind.

Like the Bible being translated into many different languages, there are many styles of music Christians use to keep their mind on God.

Images

Godly images have been used throughout our faith history to connect us to the living Christ, as well. From ancient stained glass windows and icons, to WWJD bracelets, gospel T-shirts and tattoos, visual reminders are powerful and significant. We absorb much through sight that keeps us focused on our walk with Jesus.

Mentor/Coach/Teacher/"Discipler"

Connecting with someone who is farther along on the path of self-denial, being discipled and encouraged by them, is the way Jesus designed for us to be in the process of being a disciple. Who is your Yoda?

If you are fortunate enough to have a parent in this role, that would be amazing. It can be a peer, but there is nothing like the wisdom and model of the elder who is experiencing the joy and challenge of the transforming life.

How do you find a mentor? If you are fortunate, he/she will find you. More and more church communities today are finally doing things the way Jesus designed by focusing on making disciples. You can judge a potential mentor as one who is encouraging, challenging, gracious, and confident in Jesus, and who is authentic in their walk of faith.

What is holding you back from seeking a mentor?

Instead of trying to read large amounts of the Bible as a discipline, focus on smaller passages like Colossians 3:1-7, and live there for extended periods of time.
— Dallas Willard

35. CHANGING FEELINGS

Feelings are at the front of the line when it comes to our minds. People ask "How are you feeling today?"

Has anyone ever asked you, "How are you thinking today?"

Watching the news after a terrorist attack brings an unfortunate lesson in this focus on how one feels. Newscasters ask "experts" these kind of questions:

Why do you think the terrorists feel the way they do?

What is causing them to feel that way about Western countries?

What more can we do to understand why they feel the way they do?

No one asks the obvious.

What kind of thinking is the source of such diabolical actions?

What are the ideas and images the terrorists use as their sources to fuel this type of response?

Feelings are absolutely necessary because they make us come alive and they drive our activities. We accept we have feelings and we learn to channel them in the right places and in the right way.

Feelings can be good servants but they are a horrible master.

How do we work on a vision to transform our mind's feelings?

Think of an example when you started with feelings rather than thinking.

People don't ask, "How are you thinking today?"
— *Dallas Willard*

36. FEELINGS? DON'T

Here are some ways to try to transform our feelings that don't work.

1. Trying to take on our feelings directly.

We don't know the power of feelings if we think we can just face them directly with willpower. The direct approach at changing our mind at the spur of the moment is not helpful. If we are being strongly influenced by feelings of anger, fear, sexual attraction, need for approval, ambition, and such, to just say, "Quit it!" to yourself, or to simply give in and allow your feelings to rule, "I can't help how I feel," well…No.

2. Denying our destructive feelings.

It doesn't do any good to ignore the fact we do have destructive feelings like anger, greed, jealousy, lust, and the list goes on. The Bible even has these lists in several places (e.g. Colossians 3:5-8). We can't deny we have these sinful feelings and we can't just try to keep them inside and then they will naturally go away.

3. Pouring our destructive feelings out on others.

Another way to not deal with feelings is to act them out. We don't give in to them and take it out on our others. We don't scream at someone and then think, "Now, I feel much better."

Well then, what does work?

**Think about an example
when you used one of these methods.**

> *We surrender the right to do what we want
> in favor of doing what is good under God.*
> *— Dallas Willard*

37. FEELINGS? DO

The way to transform destructive feelings is to replace them with helpful feelings. This is one of the central keys to living a transformed life. It is only under the partnership of Jesus through the power of the Holy Spirit that we can become the kind of people who lose these awful feelings, and have feelings that are helpful to others as they build us up. Here are some helpful transformation tools relating to feelings.

1. Work on feelings that move you away from sin instead of trying not to sin.

At the very earliest stages, focus on cultivating revulsion at the feelings you now have that are sinful, even if they don't bother you. Along with this, focus on being attracted strongly to feelings of good, even if you don't have those feelings to begin with.

Take anger as an example. I don't simply try to avoid feeling angry. I begin to look at how unattractive I must appear when I am angry. I focus on the sense of uneasiness I have afterwards, and the uneasiness I see in others. At the same time, I have a vision of what it is like for people to be in my presence, where they are relaxed and comfortable. Where do I bring joy?

2. Remove the underlying condition, not just the feeling.

Why do I have the destructive feelings in the first place? What are the conditions that lead up to them? Let's stay on the anger example.

What conditions lead to the anger? Perhaps it is a sense of privilege. If I think I deserve good things in my life and then they don't go my way, I am offended by my circumstances. I lash out at whoever is around me. I begin to project my disappointment on anyone whom I perceive as a source of my injustice.

It's time to move myself from the sense of privilege, and realize the whole world isn't going to end if I don't get my way.

3. Replace the underlying condition; the feelings will take care of themselves.

It isn't enough just to remove the underlying condition that fuels the destructive feelings. In the anger example, it isn't enough to try not to feel like I must always get my own way. I must replace those conditions with healthy alternatives.

One way to start is to put yourself into situations where you practice deferring to others. For example, allowing someone to pull into your traffic lane is a good place to start. If you live in an urban area, especially, you can practice this every day. Of course, the person behind you may then have to start working on their anger issues!

What is one destructive feeling you struggle with? What can you do to stop feeling that way?

If you wish to quit drinking, for example, you begin by getting rid of all the alcohol in the house.

— *Dallas Willard*

38. Feelings and Character

Change begins on the inside. This is the central place for transformation to happen. New life is possible with a change in character itself.

Character—Your internal structure that is revealed by your outward patterns of behavior.

Under times of stress and fatigue, our character reveals itself. This is not a widely known fact. We can try to live a positive, gracious image for others when things are going smoothly, but when pressure hits we can't keep up the defenses. Who we are is exposed by our circumstances.

We have some changing to do. How often do we say or do something hurtful and then apologize with this kind of line?

I have been under a lot of pressure lately.

We also see this line of thinking when someone lashes out violently and injures or kills someone. In the interview of a family member or neighbor you often hear this:

He seemed like such a nice guy. I wonder what happened to him to cause him to snap like that?

No, he was not a nice guy. Perhaps he was someone who was skilled at hiding his dominating self-worship but got caught up in circumstances where his real character was exposed.

OK, why doesn't God just force us to do good? Our freedom is what makes us so precious in God's sight. It is a key part of being created in God's image. God respects our freedom to choose. He will not force us to love him. Instead, through Jesus, God rescues us and our relationship with the Father can be restored.

We are not a lost cause. Under the power of the Holy Spirit, our true character can change for the good. This takes effort on our part, though we cannot change ourselves by the direct approach.

What excuses have you used concerning your character?

If only the Christian accountants and executives in the corporations would have followed the ways of Jesus when it came to their business practices, we wouldn't have had a Savings and Loan Crisis in our country in the first place.

— Dallas Willard

39. Help with Feelings

Here are the Bible's antidotes to destructive feelings.

Faith and hope

These go hand in hand. Faith is acting in confidence on belief based upon reality. Our reality is Jesus. As we trust in him, we are capable of seeing the future he has for us. This brings us to hope. Hope is the anticipation of good that is coming. When we combine faith and hope we act as if the good God has in store for us is already happening, because it is.

Love

Love is to will the good of others and act on it. To desire good for another and to act upon it. To make choices that bring good in someone else's life.

Love is not the same as lust, which is to desire for the sake of what we can receive. Love is giving of yourself so that other people receive benefit in their lives. Love produces the healthy feelings we are hoping for. When we are being transformed by Jesus this is what our lives look like. It is a process.

We are loved by God.

We love God.

We love others.

They experience God's love, and, therefore, love us.

A life filled with love produces feelings of love. Fear, pride, resentment and such are all dying out because we have the power of Jesus to show us we are completely safe in a life with him.

Joy

Joy is a deep sense of well being. Joy is being glad to be with God. Joy is being glad to be with others. When we have joy, we bring joy into the lives of others. Jesus means for us to have a life of joy (John 15:11). This makes it possible for us to return to joy even in times of hardship and conflict. We aren't on an emotional roller coaster, where every trouble brings feelings of fear and anxiety.

Peace

This word has two meanings.

1. To be at peace with God is to be reconciled to him through Jesus.

2. Peace is also the biblical concept of *shalom*, where we have a sense of well being based on confidence in Jesus, and know everything is going to be good even if we don't presently know exactly how.

We live in peace when we know God is in charge. That we are completely safe in God's loving arms. Then destructive feelings of anxiety and fear disappear. Not because there is no trouble and pain, but because we face everything from within the Kingdom perspective and can take the long view.

A transformed life has an environment where faith, hope, love, joy and peace can flourish.

**Whatever is troubling you recently,
what is the absolute worst thing that could happen, as
a result? What could God do if that would occur?**

We are completely safe in God's loving arms.
— *Dallas Willard*

40. Surrender and Self-Forgetfulness

God knows every person's heart. He knows how we deceive ourselves. He sees us as we are, and is ready and able to transform us. This is the only way we can be saved from ourselves. God calls us to a life of surrender, abandonment, contentment, and participation.

We surrender to God and place our complete confidence in him. If we try to hold anything back, transformation isn't possible. It's not that God couldn't change us on his own, but for the sake of our partnership he wouldn't. It's time for us to surrender.

Surrender is not a term that denotes strength, obviously. Yet, in the case of moving toward surrender by dying to yourself and your own self-worship, the one who surrenders is a giant. For years AA has used a slogan, *Let go; let God.* It is just as meaningful today.

Holding on to the me that isn't really the me God designed me to be, well, that's just plain foolish. We trust God enough to give up and now we are ready to go all the way. Abandonment means everything. Every part of who we are. We do this in fits and starts, but the more we give God from what holds us back, the more freeing this becomes.

Another word for self-denial is self-forgetfulness. Timothy Keller, is his book, *The Freedom of Self Forgetfulness*, says it this way,

> *True gospel-humility means I stop connecting every experience, every conversation, with myself. In fact, I stop thinking about myself. The freedom of self-forgetfulness. The blessed rest that only self-forgetfulness brings.*

We will then experience contentment, where we are satisfied with what we have and live lives knowing we are completely safe, immersed in God's Kingdom reality. It doesn't surprise us nor upset us when we don't get our own way. We know God will carry out his plans. Our destinies are interwoven with those plans.

When we live self-forgetful lives, we live for God and others. Then something happens on God's end. He knows he can trust us with his power. More and more he will use us to be beacons of hope and assurance in a world in desperate need of these things. What we do in our lives will look more and more like the things Jesus did when he was on earth. That's power.

It's not that God doesn't want us to have this power beforehand; it's just that without transformed hearts, power without humility can be dangerous. By transforming us, God invites us into this life of participation.

What is the greatest challenge you face? How do you want to face it?

God gives spiritual power to those he knows he can trust with it.
— Dallas Willard

41. TOOLS FOR CHANGE

Transforming the heart is the central vision of change, because the heart is where all choices are made. When you actually intend to surrender to God's will in your life, your heart will try to figure out every way possible why you can't or why you don't need to. This will come out of your own nature, fueled by the tempting of the Evil One.

This is why as you begin this heart transplant, don't expect it to be easy. It is simple to understand, but hard to do. What is necessary is to confess your need for transformation and to continue surrendering to God. In other words, repent.

Now, repentance isn't just about repenting from sin. To repent also means changing our thinking. Thinking at a new level. We repent from sin, indeed, but repenting can also mean thinking at a higher level. We change direction to new focus in our lives.

God works with us along the way, and makes it more and more possible for us to actually participate with him. There are tools God has set up for transformation. Let's look at some of these.

Silence and Solitude

Jesus went out in the desert alone.

Lord, where did you go? We couldn't find you.

Before most major decisions he makes, as recorded in the Bible, Jesus spends time alone and prays. Why?

Silence and solitude are spiritual disciplines with a rich history. Spending time alone and quiet, speaking and listening to your loving Father, is refreshment for your very soul.

When he was younger, I asked one of our sons why he thought Jesus was so fond of being alone and he said, "To get away from all the sin for awhile."

Like soldiers at war spending time alone before battle, it is good to get away for awhile. As followers of Jesus, we do battle with the forces of the Evil One.

Also with silence and solitude, we break from all the busyness of business, the ups and downs of our daily lives, and we begin to give them over to God. We are refreshed and renewed.

How do we do this? Here is one suggestion.

Start with 10 minutes or so at the end of each day, reviewing what happened. Go to a room alone or go for a walk and reflect on the day's events. Review where you may need forgiveness from God, and pray what is on your mind. Then just spend time listening. After all, you wouldn't talk to a friend about life and then when you were done, say, "OK, gotta go…" This practice may turn into more than 10 minutes, but begin here and see what happens.

When can you get away daily and spend some time with your heavenly dad?

A good measure of how you and God are doing in your life together is sitting alone in a quiet room and doing nothing.
— Dallas Willard

42. FASTING

Like other spiritual disciplines, fasting is shared by many religions. This spiritual discipline has an ample biblical witness from Moses to Jesus himself. 40 days in the wilderness being tempted by the devil is a very well known event in Jesus' life. So, what is the purpose of fasting?

Unlike fasting for political purposes, it is not to draw attention to yourself. Quite the contrary. When Jesus spoke of fasting he said,

> *Matthew 6:16*
> *And when you fast, don't make it obvious, as the hypocrites do…*

Fasting is to focus your mind, body, and spirit on Jesus. It isn't meant to be difficult or painful. In fact, according to Jesus, you may be eating anyway (John 4:32). Fasting is most often abstaining from different items of food or drink, or a period of time without any food or drink, or just without food. Throughout the ages, Christians have tried a variety of fasts. Sunup to sundown, once a week for 24 hours, even strict fasts, like twice a week fasting from eating.

When you fast, you might have cravings, and this is a good thing. When you fast you are acknowledging you don't always get what you want. This focuses your attention on Jesus, the reason for the fast. This can be a spiritually sharp time to tune in to God. It's also a time God may reveal a challenge in you which you need to address together. Take advantage of the opportunity.

Try it! I recommend a fast from dinner one night until dinner the next. During this time, still drink as it relieves dehydration headaches.
Relish the cravings...but don't eat any relish.

Fasting becomes feasting on God.
— Dallas Willard

43. WORSHIP

Evidence points to humans involved in worship for at least 30,000 years. That's the age of the oldest worship artifacts discovered by archeologists. Humans worshipped the sun, other stars, animals, even trees. While all of these are awesome creations, we know best to worship the Creator, not the creation. And the Creator is not some unknown god of nature, rather we worship the living God, revealed directly through Jesus.

When I give myself over to adoring God, it is a wonderful opportunity to get the focus off of me. This is the essence of worship. More Jesus…less me. Again, self-forgetfulness.

Where to start:

- *Attend worship*
  Make sure you worship weekly in a Christian community. The analogy of being on a team is helpful. Worship is a time set apart for us to show whose team we are on, and to encourage our teammates. Jesus lived the pattern of weekly worship. Why would I need it less?
- *Music*
  This is the heart language for most of us. Listen to

worship music. Choose the genre and artists. Currently, Hillsong United, David Crowder Band, or our own LIFEhouse worship leader, Rob Reed are my current go-to music. Fill your car, room, or iPod with music that lifts up Jesus and his glory.

- *Write down daily praises of your own in a journal*
"God, I adore you because…" "Jesus, here are reasons I worship you today…" "Holy Spirit, I am blessed by you because…"

Find time for worship today...

> *To worship Jesus includes respecting him.*
> — *Dallas Willard*

44. SERVICE

All Christians are called to love our neighbor.

"Love God, and love your neighbor," remember?

A key way for us to take loving action is through acts of compassion through the spiritual discipline of service. But this isn't the same as volunteering for a local charity. Even though volunteering for a local charity may be part of a discipline of service. If this is confusing, well, welcome to my world.

When is service a discipline, when is it a Christian response, and when is it just doing good for the sake of another person, whether you are Christian or not? See if this helps.

People serving people

God is the source of all good, so when people who don't follow Jesus serve, they do so within God's realm. Human conscience alone will lift up many opportunities to come to another's aid.

Followers of Jesus following the example of Jesus

When we follow Jesus and learn from him, we become the kind of people who serve others naturally as a response to the love we are given by him.

Service as a discipline

Intentional acts of service, focused areas of service, hidden acts of service, are all specific ways we become available for the Holy Spirit to work through us and be more open to God's power being an influence in the world.

When someone joins the armed forces, we say they are "in the service." When they are discharged it is sometimes called, "getting out."

Well, when we join Jesus in the greatest mission of the galaxies, to be used by him to expand his Kingdom, we are in the service for eternity. We never get out.

How has serving expanded you?

Service to Christ must not replace love for Christ.
— *Dallas Willard*

45. BODY CHANGE

We have now looked at the means to transform thinking. Next, we consider transformation of the body.

Our bodies are the delivery system of who we are. In a Christ-centered life, our bodies have to be ready to do what is right, and hesitant to do what is wrong. Our bodies are not evil in themselves, but they sure get us in a lot of trouble. In the process of transformation, it may be the body that gets in the way most often.

Our bodies are given to us by God as a good thing. He honors our bodies so much he chose to come in a body, as Jesus. This is called the Incarnation, literally "taking on flesh." Christianity does not teach the body is evil.

There are other faith worldviews throughout history that do teach body=bad. They also teach we have to punish our bodies (misguided Christian groups also have said this), or pretend our bodies don't exist, in order to achieve spiritual growth. There have been erroneous teachings by some Christian teachers on this topic, but is not an accurate biblical teaching.

At the same time, we don't worship our bodies or give in to bodily desires, as is called for in some other religions and philosophies. In fact, worship of the body may be one of the key worldviews of modern society. At least, it looks that way in media and advertising. Future archeologists will think of our age as the time of perfect abs, perfect butt, and all the other ways body image is portrayed.

The result of all this obsession with the body, and trying to get what we want through the body, is growing old becomes a curse. All the dieting, exercise and plastic surgery in the world is not going to erase the fact that…

…we are all going to die.

Transforming our way of thinking about our bodies brings us to the path where our body is a servant rather than the master. It is the difference between a bodily-focused life and a spiritually-focused life.

What are examples of when you were taught your body is bad?

Your body can be a good servant, but it is a terrible master.
— *Dallas Willard*

46. Body Life Don'ts

Let's look at some of the characteristics of what self-worship looks like, when our body desires take over our lives.

Self-focus

This is the natural human response to life. As Frank Sinatra reminded us,

I did it my way.

or...

I want what I want when I want it.

We may seem like two year olds who never grow up. We may allow our desires to be in charge. We just get more sophisticated in hiding the fact that we are on the throne of our own lives, instead of God.

If you want to see this attribute in action, watch how people drive in busy traffic. Cutting others off, switching lanes, driving too close—Don't think of coming into my lane!—the first five minutes of an urban commute.

It's my road and I will do whatever I want.

You can tell a tremendous amount about the character of people when you watch how they drive.

It's My Body

In order to get what I want, I allow my body to decide. The obvious result is a life of attempted physical gratification of some sort. Seeking joy or withdrawal by using booze and pills dominate the lives of many. Serial sexual activity for the young and not so young, pornography for all, modern life is not much different than the fertility religions of ancient times.

Feelings that Stimulate

Less obvious choices for giving in to our bodies have to do with other forms of pleasure or pain avoidance. Take anger, for instance.

Anger turned outward can quickly turn into rage, and anger turned inward, often turns into depression. We overlook the internal psychic pleasure of both rage and depression. The brain has a sensual response.

With rage I might shift the responsibility of my problems in life onto everyone and everything else, except, of course, on myself.

With depression, though it is often a matter of brain chemicals and wiring, there may also be times when it is a strangely comforting subconscious means to avoid taking personal responsibility to address what is making me angry.

We don't usually spend much time thinking on these things because our bodies tell us this cannot be so.

I can't help it; this is just how I feel.

Do you experience rage or depression? What happens?

Anger leads to rage which leads to contempt, which is the worst action you can have toward your neighbor.

— Dallas Willard

47. MORE BODY DON'TS

On Being a Predator

I am on the throne of my own kingdom, but that is not enough. I need to be on the throne of your life, as well. I may go into a body mode in my relationship with you.

Tongue

Verbal manipulation is where I use word games with you to try to gain advantage over you. It is a sign that our human creativity and imagination are not always a gift for the good.

Politically-correct language can be an example of this trait gone rampant. It is common tool of self-worship. Always shifting the playing field suits my purposes. Always keeping you off balance.

Other tried and true methods are whining, flattery, and repetitive requests.

Verbal attack comes into play here, as well. When I don't have the time or the interest to use principled reason, a good bitter, sarcastic, seething tongue-lashing may be a substitute I use for clear thinking.

Body Language

Here is another tool at my disposal to influence your life. I become the master of the frown, scowl, rolled eyes, crossed arms, and chin-in-the chest. I am the man of a thousand looks.

Related are the sounds of body language. Tsk, tsk's, deep sighs, and harrumph breaths come with the facial signs and gestures. Children are good at imitating adults and so they learn quickly how to join in. Just watch toddlers at play.

Remember, in all of these attempts to be the master of my own universe, you are working the same program that I am. Here is where we enter into inevitable conflict. I can't be on my throne if I have to deal with you trying to remain on yours, as well. Something has to give.

Conflict

Here is where we cross swords. All of the unholy tools I have previously mentioned may come into use. I will try to gain the advantage at all cost. After a while, it may not be getting my own way I am after, it may be just as important to me that you don't get yours. This is as old as the story of Cain and Abel (Genesis 4). If Cain is not receiving his father's blessing, well then, as a dead man, neither will Abel.

Nothing good comes from this conflict of self-worship in one person battling self-worship in another person. If the other person gives in or simply quits, your satisfaction will be short-lived. The devastating effects may be permanent.

We generally don't engage in these battles with strangers. We match up against those we love. We strike out against those with which we can least afford to have fractured relations.

A confession: After writing on these characteristics of a body-focused life rather than a spiritually-focused life, I saw myself in some of these more than I would care to admit.

How about you?

Political Correctness is a matter of desire.
— Dallas Willard

48. Body Life Do's

The vision to transform my body rests on a spiritually-focused life. Here are some characteristics of this life.

No Coercion

I don't force my ways on you. Following Jesus' way, as I am in relationship with you, I will pursue his ways. I will not try to use any forceful methods of persuasion to get you to see his ways. No coercion. I will not try to gain advantage over you. Like Jesus, I honor your capability to make your own choices without trying to manipulate you or aggressively applying pressure to make you change those choices.

Eyes on Jesus

I will be in relationship with you, but I will also pursue the ways of Jesus. As I am experiencing Christ's guidance and power in keeping my commitments to him, he is making it possible for me to refuse to follow any other road. It becomes easier to do the right thing.

In my relationship with you, if you choose a path not consistent with that of Jesus, I will respectfully decline to participate. I will do so in a gentle, non-judgmental manner, but the path I choose will be clear.

I realize this may seem strange. In the past, my decisions would be about following my own desires. It is not the past, however. It is transformation time. I am committed to following Jesus' desires. I will not try to force this on you, and neither will I back away from what he is doing in my life.

Focus

Loving God and others is my primary purpose in life. With Jesus on the throne of my life I can live this way. I am not trying to establish my kingdom, but work in his. What does this look like?

Superstar athletes learn how to mentally screen out everything that brings the possibility of the negative. Tiger Woods is an example of this. I spoke with a friend who has had the opportunity to play with many pro golfers and he said the thing that sets a Jack Nicklaus or a Tiger Woods apart from everyone else is their incredible intensity of in assessing the current situation. They live directly in the moment and always looks for something positive to tune in on before the next shot.

Hit the trees? No problem. There is that one opening there between those two big branches that make a target for the green. It is a perfect visual. If you are a golfer, you get the picture. Non-golfers, it just means these guys absolutely expect good things to happen on the course.

Arnold Palmer was once asked,

What is the most important shot in golf?

His reply?

The next one.

This is how my faith life can look. No matter what is happening around me, my body and my body language are in shalom. I can respond to any situation with the Bible's tools of positive emotion. My body responds with love, joy, peace, faithfulness, gentleness, kindness, and self-control. This is the energy I feed off in my relationships with others. Also, this creates an environment around me that reduces anxiety in others.

When are you at your best in relationships? Why do you think that is?

In my relationship with you, if you choose a path not consistent with that of Jesus, I will respectfully decline to participate.
— Dallas Willard

49. More Body Do's

Remember, when Jesus is on the throne, I am tender toward your weaknesses, even if you don't reciprocate. I offer myself to God and can be completely open to you. I can practice true tolerance.

Tolerance
Tolerance is not approving of everything you do.
The definition of tolerance is this:
I am respectful and courteous to you and I disagree with you.
You cannot be tolerant of people you agree with.

My body is living in line with Jesus and so I am relating to you through him. I am his to use as he pleases. That means I am available to you and can work for your good.

This kind of life is made possible through Jesus' sacrifice for me. As he gave his life for me, my life is totally his forever. I am the last person on earth who could ever say,

It's my body, and I will do with it what I please.

How do I actually gain this spiritually-focused life? This is about my intention, and the means I use to transform my body.

Why do you think Jesus talked so much about not being afraid and not worrying?

You cannot be tolerant of people you agree with.
— Dallas Willard

50. God Knows Best

God desires what is best for our bodies. We can have the body of Jesus. This doesn't mean that we all grow beards and look Middle Eastern!

To be changed into the likeness of Jesus means our bodies become devoted to serving God and doing what he wants done. We are created to do just this. Our health and happiness are centered on giving our bodies over to God.

Intention is critical at this point because our bodies are so demanding. So much of what gets in our way becomes an addiction. Addictions are giving in to our desires.

Jesus knows we are going to have a challenge transforming our bodies, more than anything. He said,

> *Matthew 26:41 (NLT)*
> *Keep alert and pray. Otherwise temptation will overpower you. For though the spirit is willing enough, the body is weak!*

God offers another way. We can't will ourselves to just say no. We have to place ourselves before the author and giver of life and work with him changing into our best, true selves.

What are you tempted by that is not healthy?

Addiction is about giving in to desires.
— Dallas Willard

51. GOD AND BODY

Don't idolize your body

Here is where I draw a fine line. On the one hand, having a healthy body is very helpful in giving me energy, focus, and longevity in serving God and others. On the other hand, if I get too obsessive about my body, which includes my health, I may be too anxious about death and aging and how my body may fail me. This anxiety stifles my reliance on Jesus for security.

Do you see the distinction? I am free to give my body over to Jesus, care for it through the wisdom I receive from him, and at the same time know that I will receive a new glorified body some day, and will live with him forever.

> *1 Cor. 15:43 (NLT)*
> *Our bodies now disappoint us, but when they are raised, they will be full of glory. They are weak now, but when they are raised, they will be full of power.*

Don't misuse your body

First, let's all relax. Sometimes Christians get too choosy

about this topic. Everyone seems to go to 1 Corinthians 6:19-20 to chastise someone else about something physical. It is not even used in the right context most of the time, because the "you" in these verses is plural, so it seems this is talking about the church community as the body.

> *1 Corinthians 6:19-20 (NLT)*
> *Or don't you know that your body is the temple of the Holy Spirit, who lives in you and was given to you by God? You do not belong to yourself, for God bought you with a high price. So you must honor God with your body.*

"Your body is the temple of the Holy Spirit" has been used to prohibit such things as drinking coffee, smoking, and drinking alcoholic beverages. Yet, at least in moderation, coffee and red wine, for instance, may have health benefits.

It is interesting that people don't usually use this same biblical passage for exercise and proper diet. When a preacher talks about the body being a temple of the Holy Spirit and criticizes only certain things, it may be that his temple has a big front porch hanging over his belt, though he doesn't smoke or drink alcohol…

It is important for us to have a healthy diet and exercise. It is important for us to get enough rest. In America especially, we are really susceptible to being overworked, overweight, undernourished and sleep deprived. Transforming our bodies includes all of this.

The other ways we can misuse our bodies I have already addressed. Trying to be sexually alluring, power dressing, body language, verbal manipulation, and such. We are to give ourselves over to Jesus, as we are now his body.

You are the body of Christ...

Why are we always so interested in the personal habits of others?

If you misuse your body don't beat yourself up over it, rather go back to vision, intention, and means.

— *Dallas Willard*

52. A Body Experiment

Romans 12:1 (NLT)
And so, dear brothers and sisters, I plead with you
to give your bodies to God. Let them be a living and
holy sacrifice—the kind he will accept. When you
think of what he has done for you, is this too much
to ask?

You have to be absolutely clear why you owe your body life to God. I am afraid that when Paul asks the question, "Is this too much to ask?" most of us are saying, "Yes it is."

Do you really understand that God is in charge of your desires and your pleasures? Then release them to him.

One way you can accomplish this, with the partnership of the Holy Spirit, is to join God in an experiment. What is a body sin that is challenging you? Is it anger, gossip, pornography, unhealthy eating?

Whatever it is, don't do it for one day.

It will look something like this.

Get up in the morning. Realize how good God is and thank him for this. Tell God you are dedicating this day to him. Think of the the one body sin you want to get rid of. Give this to Jesus for the day. Make a commitment to him.

For example,

Jesus, today I will not gossip.

This means your texting, Facebook posts, Tweets, phone calls or conversations may be a little boring for the day. It doesn't matter. You are following old advice.

Unless you have something nice to say about someone, don't say anything at all.

Quaint, but effective.

When you are tempted to gossip, you will think of Jesus instead. You can't imagine him going,

Hey John, did you hear Peter last night? "Lord, I will never leave you." What a loser. Peter is so full of himself!

Think of a reporter following you everywhere you go this day. Taping every word. Now realize this is exactly what is happening. The reporter is Jesus and he is right next to you. Now.

Really.

One day.

Try it out.

Then go to bed.

Wake up and start over.

Is there a bad habit you want to break? Go for it!

If you conscientiously try out just one of Jesus' teachings
he will reveal himself to you.
— Dallas Willard

53. Body Life of Jesus

My body is from God, and since he sent Jesus to set me free from sin and death, my body is not mine. It is claimed by Jesus and he uses it here and now. It is helpful to join Jesus in some of the ways he addressed the challenge of his body.

Followers of Jesus discover it is a good thing to stop and reflect on what God is doing. Celebrate how good God is. You can do this daily, weekly, and yearly.

Take silence and solitude time each day to break from whatever is going on around you.

Once a week, spend a day in reflection of God and enjoy him through those around you. For many, Sunday is this time of connecting to God, family, and friends.

Once a year you might spend several days away from your normal routine and just do nothing. There is more to rest than sleep. God rested (Genesis 2:2). Jesus rested (Matthew 14:13). Jesus invites us to abide in him (John 15).

Dedicate the proper care of your body to Jesus

When you diet, exercise, and get enough sleep, your physical health improves. It is good for your emotional well being.

It is good for your soul. When you do these things with Jesus in mind, he can choose to be part of the process. You are inviting him to be a partner. Use Vision/Intention/Means with your dieting, exercise and sleep. This can be very helpful.

What is one thing you can add to your life for the good of your body?

I think I'll just have oatmeal.
— Dallas Willard

54. Social Relations

The transformation up to this point has been about us, personally. Heart, mind, and body.

Heart—our will; the choices we make

Mind—thoughts and feelings

Body—our physical presence through which we live out our lives

But...

"It is not good that the man should be alone..." (Genesis 2:18)

We are created in community. It is how we are wired. God intends for us to be in relationship with him and other people. The idea that we are to go it alone, or stick to ourselves is not a biblical concept. The Bible is filled with descriptions of living in community. We even know God as community. The Trinity. Father, Son, and Holy Spirit.

We are created to live with other people. The challenge is I am a sinful person and it is absolutely necessary that I am in relationship with others, who, yes, are sinful people. It doesn't take too long for us to realize this is going to be messy.

Adam and Eve start arguing right away.

What did God say?

Then, when they sin by doing what God forbids, Adam blames Eve. Eve blames the devil. When their children are born it doesn't get any easier. Eventually Cain kills his brother Abel.

And so it goes.

Living with others is absolutely essential for our spiritual, physical, and emotional well being, and living with others can be absolutely harmful to our spiritual, physical, and emotional well being.

We can't live in healthy community with each other, unless Jesus is on the throne of our lives. Without Jesus, my self-worship and your self-worship are always going to result in a disconnect at some point.

What's the answer? God's way.

Dream of what your friendships would be like if you were a friend like Jesus.

As human beings, we are designed to be connected to others.
— Dallas Willard

55. GOD AND SOCIAL RELATIONS

Unbutu. A person is a person through other persons.
—*Bishop Desmond Tutu*

Unbutu is a Swahili word that draws our attention to the fact that we are dependent on each other. Often, the concept of a circle is used to illustrate this.

Who is in your circle?

Draw a big circle and place in it the names of the people in your life. This circle tells you something about your social relationships. Are there many people or few?

If there are many, who are you in close relationship with? Many psychologists think you can really be in a close, intimate relationship with very few people, perhaps only one other. Do you have any of these soul mates in your circle?

If there are only a few people in your circle to begin with, why do you think that's the case? If your circle is filled with names, how close are you, really, to them? There are a lot of things to consider.

When we look at our circle, realize God desires good to come out of it. As we are connected in healthy ways, this will happen.

In order for our circles to be life-giving, we are connected to each other in healthy ways. This is no easy connection.

If we follow our own human nature, we continue to move away from each other in our circles. In self-worship, we are the only occupants who really count.

Start praying for people in your circle.

God's forgiveness of us is contingent on our forgiving each other.
— *Dallas Willard*

56. SOCIAL RELATIONS DON'TS

There are two actions that wreck social relationships more than any other. Attack and withdrawal.

Attack

To verbally and/or physically be aggressive toward someone with the intent of using this as a means to get our own way or to at least punish the other people.

Withdrawal

To ignore someone. Hide ourselves and our feelings from them. Act as if we don't care at all. All the way to holding them in contempt, as if they don't even exist in our mind at all. These are all passive ways to try to control or punish.

We use attack and withdrawal so much we think they are are as normal as breathing and we couldn't think of life without them. Actually, we will not have a transformed life with them.

If we are to live in our circle of life with actions for the good, we need to eliminate attack and withdrawal. If we desire to expand our circle we need to get rid of attack and withdrawal from our own lives. Let's be clear on what is at stake.

Attack is when we act against the good of other people. We are doing what we can to make sure they don't prosper for the moment, or longer. Attack may be launched for the right reasons, as in the case of trying to correct unhealthy behavior in someone else, but it is the wrong method. Screaming at your children because they aren't doing their homework comes to mind.

Attack is certainly addressed by God in the Bible. The Ten Commandments, from "Honor your father and mother" on, are about our relationships, and they all address attack in some way.

Withdrawal is working against the good of other people, as well. But, instead of visibly attacking them, we hide, or we ignore them, or we reach the point of despising them. Treating them as if they don't exist.

Quick current examples:

Attack—Watch political debate in Congress on CSPAN (Cable-Satellite Public Affairs Network) for two minutes.

Withdrawal—Watch the relationship between teenagers and their parents on just about any TV show or in any movie.

Do you tend to use attack or withdrawal in your relationships?

To have contempt for someone is to act as if they don't exist at all.
— *Dallas Willard*

57. How God Heals Relations

The healing of our circle of relationships is connection to God. God is a healthy community in God's self. We know God as Father, Son, and Holy Spirit. The Trinity is the model of healthy, loving, social relationships.

Within the Trinity, there is no attempt to control or seek one's own way. They show deference to one another within the Trinitarian community because Father, Son and Holy Spirit won't stand for lording it over another.

The Trinity shows us we are created to live in community.

Created in God's image (Genesis 1:26-27), we are at our best when we join God in this community of love.

We can be free from the positioning and posturing of making a place for ourselves in our relationships.

The legend of King Arthur and his Round Table is a good illustration of this.

The story goes, Arthur wanted his knights to consider themselves as no better than the other. He as King saw himself in this same light. In order to symbolize this community of deferring to the other, he had a round table built for them, so there would never be anyone at the head of the table when they came together.

The key to living transformed lives in community with others is not a mystery. No one is more special than you in the eyes of God. No one is less special than you. The difficulty is not in the understanding, but in the follow through. If you wish to have a life filled with richness in your relationships, that's where you start.

> *Philippians 2:3-5 (NLT)*
> *Don't be selfish; don't live to make a good impression on others. Be humble, thinking of others as better than yourself. Don't think only about your own affairs, but be interested in others, too, and what they are doing. Your attitude should be the same that Christ Jesus had.*

As we are transformed by God to become the kind of people God can work through, we take on the mind of Jesus. We begin to think as he thinks. Our actions, then, reflect his influence. We live in our circle of relationships as Jesus lives in the circle of the Trinity. We bring Jesus with us to our own Round Table because he is in us and we are in him.

> *1 John 4:15-16 (NLT)*
> *All who proclaim that Jesus is the Son of God have God living in them, and they live in God. We know how much God loves us, and we have put our trust in him. God is love, and all who live in love live in God, and God lives in them.*

How have you viewed the Trinity and how does seeing God living in relationship help?

Living in his Kingdom we move from having faith in Jesus to having the faith of Jesus.
— *Dallas Willard*

58. MARRIAGE

The central place for social relations to have impact is in families and extended families. This is the fertile foundation for all other relationships both for good and evil. Family, those you live with, can be the most common place for attack and withdrawal, but it can also be a place where you learn mutual submission for the sake of the other. Where you can actually become Christlike in a way that is matchless. Transformation is a long view process that begins and continues with those closest to you.

Marriage is the place where God designed us to be at our most intimate and our most vulnerable. Husbands and wives are created to complement each other, as well as compliment each other.

This is why I have modeled and taught the biblical model of marriage from day one with our children. I encourage them to know that some day they will most likely join someone in holy matrimony, and their lives will be enhanced for all their days on earth.

Genesis 2:18 (NLT)
And the LORD God said, "It is not good for the man

to be alone. I will make a companion who will help him."

The word for "companion" or "helper" in other versions of the Bible, can also be translated from the Hebrew as, "one who sees things from a different perspective."

Husbands and wives are created to see things differently. Marriage becomes a place where the giving of ourselves for the sake of the other is best practiced by God's design. And in marriage, husband and wife are constantly tested.

When they have children, parents then become the model. The very best and the very worst models of what it means to live in community usually starts right there in the home. You can't experience transformation of your relationships outside of your family, without the foundation of transformation within your family.

Here is the challenge. A family is made up of individuals who are naturally moving toward self-worship. Society caters to this narcissistic focus of—what's in it for me?

As a result of proximity, family relationships are especially fragile. So much is at stake. Alienation and contempt may become common place. Divorce may seem the only way out for marriages. Parents and children may look upon each other as enemies.

There is another way.

You can invite the community of Father, Son, and Holy Spirit to join with you. You can begin to live in God's ways and declare a no attack and no withdrawal zone as it relates to you. No matter what your family relationships are, you can become the new generation who will birth a new community of love for years to come.

What is the relationship between marriage and discipleship?

> *"Love your neighbor as yourself"*
> *and your spouse is your closest neighbor.*
> — *Dallas Willard*

59. FAMILIES INFLUENCE SOCIETY

Being personally transformed in our lives, our families and extended families are influenced. As our families and extended families are transforming, we influence the community around us. There are times in Christian history when transformation becomes so powerful that whole communities change.

Consider the Welsh Revival. In 1904 there was an intentional spiritual reawakening that swept through Wales. The country itself was changed. Taverns were emptied. There were days when the courtrooms were empty. Even animals were affected.

There is the story of the small ponies the Welsh miners used to move their coal cars underground. These ponies started messing up on the job.

It seems they were so used to the curses of their masters, that when the miners stop swearing, the ponies didn't understand the commands, and didn't know how to follow them!

The ideal in our circle of life is to join God and love like he loves in his Trinity. Then through our love of God, we love others in our circle the same. Then they join God as well, and love us back, and all of our lives are enriched as a result. Together, then, we share this love outside the circle, and we impact the wider community.

We are not so naive as to expect everyone will give love after receiving it. This includes those in our circle of influence, as well as outside it.

Yet, we are energized to love as Christ loves whether it is returned or not. Love expands us. To be in God's will is a blessed place.

Are there ways you have recently been an influence for good in your own family/extended family? Think about this.

It starts with loving God as our first love.
— Dallas Willard

60. Put on Christ

The first means I use to transform my social relations is to put on Christ. My Heavenly Father gives me my identity through Jesus.

Perhaps you are familiar with identity theft. This is where someone steals your credit card numbers and/or social security number and begins to make purchases under your name. Sometimes making large transactions as if they were you. There are safeguards to prevent this crime and to protect my identity.

Yet, in the big picture, my true identity is not my Social Security number. My identity is given to me by God. I am the beloved son of the loving Father. He's my dad! You're his son or daughter, too! We are secure.

To start with this identity, it makes it possible to live a life of self-denial, or self-forgetfulness, and live a life of service toward others. This makes it possible to forgive others and bless them rather than curse. This is a new life.

Col. 3:10 (NLT)
In its place you have clothed yourselves with a brand-new nature that is continually being renewed as you

learn more and more about Christ, who created this new nature within you.

What would it be like for people to say of you, "You are like a new person!" Dwell on this.

God is available to his children.
— Dallas Willard

61. LOSING THE MASKS

Another means to transform social relations is to lose the masks we wear. We present ourselves as authentically as possible.

Attack and withdrawal result in our setting up huge walls against being vulnerable. We are likely to put on masks to hide who we are, because we don't like who we are, and we don't want others to see our darker side. Or, we wear masks in order to look better and achieve recognition and reward for being someone we are not.

This is especially tempting in a church community. We have one mask for our Christian friends and one mask for our day-to-day life.

Another mask we may choose to wear is to be following Jesus, but hiding our love for him so we don't appear too religious to our friends. This seems strange, but sometimes Christians may show signs of real vulnerability and growth within their Christian community, but intentionally try to look like someone else at work or school.

For a follower of Jesus all masks must go. There is no hiding in humility.

Now, this doesn't mean that our lives become therapy sessions with each other. It's not about being brutally honest or baring our souls. It's about being in relations where we can be who we are, not attempting to hide that, and it's about joining with God together so we might be who he intends for us to be through him.

That's why we need to be in community with other followers of Jesus. It is the model of Jesus to be open and honest in life together with his family and extended family. We follow him when we hold each other accountable to be real with the people around us. Our public and private lives begin to match. We give up using deceit, coercion, manipulation and defensiveness in our relationships. Our identity comes from God, and he makes it possible for us to face the world unmasked, making progress as our best, true selves.

What mask is ready to come off of you now?

People were drawn to the real Jesus.
— Dallas Willard

62. EXPANDING LOVE IN RELATIONS

Let genuine love rule.

Romans 12:9-10 (NLT)
Don't just pretend that you love others. Really love
them. Hate what is wrong. Stand on the side of the
good. Love each other with genuine affection, and
take delight in honoring each other.

If I am following the model of Jesus, I am not going to put on a false act when I am with you, and then have another attitude behind your back.

If someone is a challenge to you, it gives you a chance to expand your character. You stretch your potency when you desire to bless someone who doesn't necessarily wish to bless you back. When I am being transformed, I love you like Jesus loves you. I desire you to be blessed and I act upon this. I value you, as a son or daughter of the same Father!

Genuine love builds up rather than tears down. This means I try to catch you at your best. As a loving person, I do this automatically. I do not make attempts to put you on the defensive, where you are less likely to respond graciously. There is a phrase used that sums these actions up:

Anxiety-producing behavior.

Anxiety-producing behavior occurs when I try to produce anxiety in people on purpose, to somehow advance my own agenda, or gain more attention to my rightness. It may be subtle or even unconscious, but it is there. I may exaggerate the negative.

Genuine love takes the time to know what is necessary to put people at ease, even when dealing with conflict and disagreement. As a loving person, you are not pushy or aggressive. Instead, you practice wide boundaries of graciousness.

"Love is seeking the good of another."
What does this mean to you?

Love is not something you choose to do but what you choose to be.
— *Dallas Willard*

63. LOVE EXPANDS THROUGH RELATIONS

Pay it forward.

This is another important tool for the transformation of our relationships. The movie, *Pay it Forward* brings the concept out in a powerful way. The film is about what might happen if you reach out for the sake of another and then they do the same.

Do something unusually good for someone else, and then tell them they have to do something good for three other people who do it for three other people, and so on. In other words, you can't return the good deed; you have to pay it forward.

When the film was released, movie critics didn't buy it.

Here is what Roger Ebert had to say,

That's the theory behind "Pay It Forward," a movie that might have been more entertaining if it didn't believe it. It's a seductive theory, but in the real world, altruism is less powerful than selfishness, greed, nepotism, xenophobia, tribalism and paranoia. If you doubt me, take another look at the front pages.

I would have two responses to the review.

1. Have you ever tried it?

2. Have you actually studied the lives of those who have

tried it?

It's not that willing the good of your neighbor and taking action on it, loving your neighbor, in other words, can't be done. It's just that I don't do it or I am not in relations in a community where this happens.

When I take Jesus at his word, love expands.

John 15:10-12 (NLT)
I have loved you even as the Father has loved me.
Remain in my love. When you obey me, you remain
in my love, just as I obey my Father and remain in
his love. I have told you this so that you will be filled
with my joy. Yes, your joy will overflow! I command
you to love each other in the same way that I love
you.

In other words, the love Jesus experiences in the Trinity, is given to me, and I pay it forward to someone else, who in turn will be influenced by my action, and will have the opportunity to pay it forward to others. If you have God working through you, you will never run out of love.

Apologies to Roger Ebert, but this theory does work in the real world.

The real world is where God rules, God's Kingdom. If all the parties involved are being changed by the Holy Spirit and living transformed lives, then to pay it forward is as natural as selfishness is in a world that doesn't recognize the transforming power of God.

As we reach out in love to others, and they are under the same power of the Holy Spirit, they will bless us, as well as bless others. Can you imagine what it will be like if we all live in communities where people are transformed followers of Jesus? Pay it forward will be no big deal. Such communities do exist and we can live in such a community.

It starts with you.

When did you do something loving for someone and saw them pay it forward. How did that make you feel?

You can't say you believe in Jesus if you don't think he is right about everything.

— Dallas Willard

64. Soul Transformation

When we think of soul, there are three main ways to think of it.

1. The soul is a vague characteristic of something we either have or we don't.

He's got soul. She's got soul.

2. The soul is an immaterial entity that is contained within us.

I love you down to my very soul.

3. The soul doesn't exist at all.

We are completely physical, and any other sense of who we are comes from electrical impulses in our brain circuitry and chemical reactions. It's just how we are wired.

There is another way.

4. The soul is beyond our body.

The soul contains the body, but it is much bigger than that. Our soul is the organizing force that holds together heart, mind, body, and social relations. The soul is the CEO of who we are.

If the soul organizes us, then it is given to us at conception, and through it God creates and organizes our DNA and all the life that follows.

This may seem strange, but let's say it is true that we are organized by our soul. If my soul is real and is the glue that holds my life together, then I am missing out on absolutely key knowledge of what it means to be human if I don't know about my soul.

Yet, that is exactly the case today. The reality of the soul is not a standard course of study in high school, at the university, or even in churches nowadays. So, let's consider the soul.

**Another way the soul has been explained is,
"The soul is like the captain of a ship."
What does this look like to you?**

Our soul is given to us at conception.
— Dallas Willard

65. Soul or Spirit?

What is the difference between the human soul and human spirit?

Think of the car.

The "spirit" is the interface between the driver and the car. The steering wheel, door locks, GPS and such. Things we consciously operate.

The "soul" is the computer system behind it all. We don't directly connect with the computer. The soul regulates and organizes, and then the spirit takes action on the decisions. In all of this, hopefully, it is God who is in charge of the driver!

As the soul is the organizer, the soul needs to function well in order for the rest of the parts of who I am to work well. When I am using my whole self in any endeavor of life, a healthy soul is absolutely essential.

A healthy soul brings health to all aspects of my life. In our time, many of our most respected thinkers have dismissed the concept of the soul and its importance in integrating our lives in healthy ways. So, how's it going, as a result?

Look at some of these basic aspects of human life and you tell me. One example is sleep.

According to Archibald Hart, in *The Anxiety Cure*, half of all adult Americans suffer from some form of insomnia. Without a good night's sleep, everything else is affected.

Or take sex.

Is it is a private, intimate bonding experience for husbands and wives where two become one, on occasion bringing about new life for the next generation? Is that the purpose of sexual relations as designed by God? If so, how are we doing?

Marriage,
      parenting,
           work,
                friendships,
                    love of neighbor—

how are we doing??

If we say it is only a material world and we are simply particles and progress, then what is exactly is life?

If you deny the soul, you still have to get up in the morning and live life. Real life.

Meaning and purpose are essential ingredients of a healthy life. Where are they located in the material worldview?

Fortunately, we don't have to buy into the despair of hopelessness, meaninglessness, and skepticism that has been such a staple in certain circles for the last 150 years. We just need to get to the soul of the matter, and fortunately, more and more people are willing to have a look.

If the real world is actually the unseen spiritual world, then what does the phrase, "get real," actually mean? Think about this.

If you deny the soul, you still have to get up in the morning and live life.

— Dallas Willard

66. Healing the Soul

God is in charge. He is the source of transformation and he doesn't hide this from us. The Bible is the way God gives us the plan to heal our souls. This begins and ends with the fact that we don't trust in our own wisdom, we trust in God's.

God's wisdom comes through the pages of the Bible filtered through our interaction with him. Without biblical wisdom under the power of the Holy Spirit, we are left with two choices to guide and transform our lives.

1. We are the source of what will transform our lives for the good.
2. Understanding based on something other than a biblical worldview will transform our lives for the good.

Here are the challenges of either of these viewpoints.

1. If I am the source of transformation in my life, then I know there is great risk, because I have been wrong before and I can't imagine that I am not going to be wrong again.

2. As far as other worldviews go, no matter how brilliant the thinking may be, if it is not filtered through the Scripture, it can't always be trusted.

Sure, it may be an identical principle, as Jesus is the source of all truth. Truth is truth and so we can expect to find good, solid teaching in other religions and worldviews. Yet, how do we know if the teaching veers away from God's Word if we don't know the Bible?

God gives people a conscience to guide them, whether they know the Bible or not, but we can ignore our consciences so easily. Human history is filled with the disaster of people doing what they know is wrong, and then convincing themselves that it is not wrong after all, or even worse, relishing the evil behavior.

For those who trust God's Word, these are less likely to be options. An honest assessment of world history reveals this.

Transformation of the soul occurs through those who love the Word. They read the Bible in a careful, straightforward manner, and live it day to day. This is not usually a huge leap in life change, but rather a slow, quiet exposure to the Word of Life.

Read Ephesians, and then think about why reading the Bible is a key part of transformation.

If you honestly think you have found a better way to live your life
than following the Kingdom life of Jesus—go for it
…and good luck.
— Dallas Willard

67. Soul Work

If I choose to live by my own desires, my life is headed for ruin. Unfortunately, this is the natural path of human beings. We don't have to learn how to do this. Transformation is not necessary.

But, fortunately, God is brilliant enough to design life circumstances that kick in whether we follow him or not. Things are always changing.

If I am married, I begin to see that my way isn't always the way it is. If we have children, this is even more evident. When I learn that I am not in charge of my life, it is a good start.

It isn't a shock that research shows that being married with children brings about greater physical and emotional health than any other social arrangement. Without living on a deliberate path of self-forgetfulness and being transformed, from a human standpoint, married with children is the best chance we get. Yet, we know, marriage and parenthood are not enough.

To live intentionally, focusing on transformation of all the parts of who I am, is the means to long-term health, and through Jesus, the means to eternal significance. We don't have to wait to get married and have kids to begin this process. It can start any day, and at any time in our lives. The soul is at the center of the whole endeavor.

We join Jesus in transforming our hearts, minds, bodies, and social relations. The soul integrates all of these and makes our life, our life, for the first time. We can actually live life the way we are designed. I think of Michael Jordan as an example of this.

The Bulls had Michael Jordan for a couple of years before they started winning championships. They didn't become the world famous Chicago Bulls until Michael learned how to involve the other four players and integrate them fully in the game.

When he was great on his own, they won, but no championships. When he became the catalyst who led all five players working together toward the common purpose of winning, things clicked. Six championships! Not isolated from the parts, but integral to organizing the whole.

In a way, Michael functioned like our soul, making sure everyone was involved and contributing in a healthy way.

Ultimately, it is this transformation of the soul that God desires to accomplish. If I am to make any headway, and the soul is, indeed, at the center of who I am, then it is critical to think deeply about my soul.

The key starting point is to realize I am not contained in my body. I am not only a physical being. I am not a human being having a spiritual experience. I am a spiritual being having a human experience.

True knowledge is not measured by lab instruments. True knowledge starts with realizing the physical is not all there is.

Just like the physical body, the soul needs proper care. The soul lasts forever. It is not a ghost that leaves our body and floats around after we die. The soul is not physical and limited to our body's boundaries, it is a non-physical reality.

Caring for the soul centers on the spiritual disciplines which bring refreshment to our existence. Our souls are grievously damaged over the years. Abuse, betrayal, abandonment, and other destructive forces in our lives chip away at our identity and rob us of the joy God has for us always. Our souls are bruised and broken. We need God to renew us. We need God to heal us. We need God to make us new.

We give ourselves over to God's care.

Think of the similarity between team work and soul work.

> *We can become the kind of people*
> *who can do the good automatically.*
> — *Dallas Willard*

68. Jesus is Ready

Matthew 11:28-30 (NLT)
Then Jesus said, "Come to me, all of you who are
weary and carry heavy burdens, and I will give you
rest. Take my yoke upon you. Let me teach you, be-
cause I am humble and gentle, and you will find
rest for your souls. For my yoke fits perfectly, and the
burden I give you is light."

In Jesus' day, a yoke is a wooden harness that is used in agriculture to put two oxen together so they can work together pulling a load or plowing a field. The system works best when you take an experienced older ox and yoke him to an inexperienced younger one. The younger ox learns to follow the lead of the older, and the older teaches the younger to share the load. After a while, the oxen work together as one.

Jesus invites you to be yoked to him. In this way he can teach you to live your life as he would live it if he were you, and he actually guides you, as you are yoked to his lead.

You are no longer working on your strength, but his; not your direction, but his direction. In this way, you are able to succeed in the way he desires in every area of transformation.

Who would actually make a yoke in Jesus' day? Interesting…

> *His yoke is light and easy.*
> *— Dallas Willard*

69. READY AND WILLING

God is not doing great things in the world to make it possible for us to receive accolades. It's not as if God starts his day declaring,

"This morning I am going to make sure that everyone knows how wonderful Dana is. I want all eyes on him. Let's see, what can I do to make sure he gets affirmation?"

It is enough to know God has me in mind, at all. Yet, it is more than that. I know he does think I am precious, regardless of what others think. I know I am the apple of his eye. His confidence in me makes me want to give my life to him. Sinful as I am, it is still bits and pieces of my life, but I am moving in his direction, yoked to Jesus.

How about it?

The essence of a transformed life is where God's Word is taken into your very soul and becomes a way of life. Are you ready?

It is not as if the Bible is simply one of many sources for all that is necessary to lead a healthy and complete existence, fully immersed in the reality of God's Kingdom. The Bible is the only source.

It always fascinates me, when, even the most conscientious people, seek other paths rather than Jesus and his Word. Usually, they haven't even given him a try!

It is interesting that there are many teachings in modern times that come directly from the Bible that are considered quite helpful, but people don't realize it's from the Bible. When you see some teaching out there that has proved in the long run to be very helpful, I'll bet you don't have to dig too far to discover it comes out of biblical principles.

In modern history, for example, we have all the recovery movements, beginning with AA. These are all steeped in biblical principles. Huge business book best sellers like *Seven Habits of Highly Effective People* by Stephen Covey, or any of the many books by Ken Blanchard and John Maxwell, are all based on biblical principles.

I am not saying that all of these examples, or others like them, are 100% pure Bible. I am saying that they are based on key biblical teachings that have actually proven to be helpful for the long term. Even people unaware of the source make progress when biblical principles are being lived out.

Here's a test for anyone. Intentionally and honestly follow just one teaching of Jesus for an extended period of time, let's say, six weeks.

The truth is, even if you only follow one teaching, if you are consistent and honest about it, he will draw you to all else that is necessary for you to come to confident faith in him. If you are open to him.

You will begin to learn from him to have faith in him. Start any time. One teaching. "Do not seek revenge." "Pray for those who persecute you." "Don't worry." Whatever the teaching, start with one.

Have you actually tried to live one teaching of Jesus? Have you actually incorporated this into your life? Until a conscious, obedient effort is made to let Jesus guide you in a specific arena of your life, it doesn't make any sense to say, "I can't do this," or "It won't work for me."

Spend some time reading Psalm 119.
Soak in the rhythm of respect given to God's ways.

Jesus is certainly the most intelligent human being
who ever lived on earth.
— *Dallas Willard*

70. God's in Charge

Key to all talk of transformation is to recognize we are not responsible for the results. God is in charge of results.

We partner with Jesus, arranging and rearranging our lives to learn from him, and we work with him, any way possible. But, when it comes to outcomes, these are solely in Jesus' hands.

This is such a freeing way to look at life. It's like the biblical parables of farming. We plant and wait.

No manipulation.

No yelling at the seed to get growing.

We simply follow the faithful work Jesus is working through us and we watch…and we wait…

This takes a large dose of humility.

1 Peter 5:5-7 (NLT)
You younger men, accept the authority of the elders.
And all of you, serve each other in humility, for
"God sets himself against the proud,
but he shows favor to the humble."

> *So humble yourselves under the mighty power of God, and in his good time he will honor you. Give all your worries and cares to God, for he cares about what happens to you.*

Why do so many pastors dread hospital visits? They pray with patients, but rarely do they see healing. At least healing that is miraculous. So, they become discouraged. It ought not be so.

First, there are many ways healing occurs. At the moment, in time, or when a person dies and eternal healing takes place.

Second, people can get better and make progress with their illness or disease. Healing is almost always a process. Prayer fuels this.

Third, and most important to remember. God is in charge of the results. We simply pray. The rest is up to him.

Pray for someone's healing in a way that expects the healing to already be taking place.

God is in charge of results.
— Dallas Willard

Afterword

(It is beyond coincidence that I was editing this page on this very day. Dallas died this morning, and is now fully healed and at rest with the Lord. A great warrior is receiving a hero's welcome in the heavenly dimensions!)

We have spent much time examining a vision of what it can mean to live a transformed life. As we have the intention to make this a reality, we have been given the means to follow through.

If you have been following the progress of change of the five parts of who you are, if you have been practicing what you are reading, you are well on your way.

If you haven't begun yet, and just considered this book a quick read, return to the beginning and actually try living this out.

Reboot.

God's desire for you since before the beginning of time is that you would come to him in complete transparency and say, "Yes," to him and all his ways.

I leave you with these words from an important song in my journey, and I pray to God you will join me on the same path:

Just like King David I cry out to You
Create in me a clean heart
I've grieved You again I need Your release
From patterns that keep me in sin
But there's only one way I can finally break free
Change me on the inside…

"Change Me On The Inside" CCLI Song No. 2956367
© 2000 Vineyard Songs Canada (Admin. by Music Services)
Brian Doerksen

About the Author

Dana Hanson is husband to Nancy, father to Kristina (Sean Herman), Gregory, and David, and grandfather to Kaylee. He was a personal student and friend of Dallas Willard for over 12 years. Dana has lived in the Los Angeles area for over 30 years, serving as pastor of a local Lutheran church, LIFEhouse Church of Northridge CA, for all that time!

Dana is the creator of the How To Be A Christian Without Being A Jerk! series, endorsed by Dallas Willard, a veteran blogger (danahanson.org, grandpablogger.com), who has worked with Faithinkubators in parenting and the faith/ science field, and 3DM in discipleship training.

Born in Wisconsin, Dana continues to be an avid Badger and Packer fan. He enjoys coaching boy's high school varsity basketball, golf, weightlifting, hiking, and family vacations in Maui. Friday is his favorite day because it's Grandpa Day, when he gets to watch Kaylee!